UNDER THE
"MUHLBERRY" TREE

From the Artist about the Cover

Mrs. Muhl took students who were "blank canvases" (the white of the cover) and added "color" to their lives, represented by the grass and sky. Her wisdom and knowledge, shown as the "Muhlberry" tree, can be seen clearly through the black-framed window, allowing all who know her and all who "enter" this book to experience her influence for the rest of their lives.

—Cathy Hall

UNDER THE "MUHLBERRY" TREE

A TEACHER REMEMBERS

LINDA MUHL

SUNSTONE PRESS

SANTA FE

Sunstone books may be purchased for educational, business,
or sales promotional use. For information please write:
Special Markets Department, Sunstone Press,
P.O. Box 2321, Santa Fe, New Mexico 87504-2321.

Book and Cover design ›Vicki Ahl
Body typeface › Minion Pro and Trajan Pro
Printed on acid free paper

Library of Congress Cataloging-in-Publication Data

Muhl, Linda, 1937-
   Under the "muhlberry" tree : a teacher remembers / by Linda Muhl.
      p. cm.
   Includes bibliographical references.
   ISBN 978-0-86534-741-0 (softcover : alk. paper) -- ISBN 978-0-86534-742-7
(hardcover : alk. paper)
   1. Muhl, Linda, 1937- 2. High school teachers--Texas--Mesquite--Biography.
I. Title.
   LA2317.M843 2009
   373.110092--dc22
   [B]
                                        2009040744

WWW.SUNSTONEPRESS.COM
SUNSTONE PRESS / POST OFFICE BOX 2321 / SANTA FE, NM 87504-2321 /USA
(505) 988-4418 / ORDERS ONLY (800) 243-5644 / FAX (505) 988-1025

DEDICATION

To my husband, Drew, who made my teaching career possible
and who loves me and all of our family unconditionally,

To my sister, Nan, who has been and always will be
my role model as a person as well as a teacher,

To my children and their spouses,
whose love, respect, and attention comfort me,

To my grandchildren, who make me a proud grandmother,

To my soul sisters, Gay and Lynne, who keep me sane and
cheerful, and

To all my students who gave me their attention and
who continue to voice their loyalty and love,

THIS BOOK IS FOR YOU!

CONTENTS

FOREWORD_____11

PREFACE_____15

I
JUST ME _____17

"A Dream Deferred" _____ 19

My Work Ethic _____ 26

An Ideal Life _____ 29

My Favorite Things _____ 33

II
DECISIONS, DECISIONS _____39

To Substitute or Not to Substitute? _____ 41

Middle or High? That was the Question._____ 45

III
UNEXPECTED PERKS _____49

Life-long Learning 1 _____ 51

Life-long Learning 2 _____ 53

Sharing Talents _____ 55

Happiness, Better Known as "Supreme and Lasting Joy" ___ 58

Supporting Community Service _____ 62

Playing Cupid _____ 66

A Dove on My Shoulder _____ 69

Bleeding Green _____ 72

Laughter, the Best Medicine _____ 74

IV
BASE CURRICULUM _____ 77

Teaching Vocabulary _____ 79

Teaching Grammar _____ 83

The Vanishing Art of Letter Writing _____ 86

Leadership Training _____ 88

Adding Social Studies . . . _____ 92

History Lessons from Fiction _____ 95

Why Focus on Art? _____ 98

Life Lessons from Literature _____ 104

With Friendship Comes Responsibility _____ 108

Just Tripping Along _____ 110

Money, Money Everywhere _____ 119

Special Activities, Projects, and Products Over the Years __ 122

V
SIDE DISHES _____ 127

Sponsoring Cheerleading _____ 129

The Birthing of Senior Mentorship _____ 132

Setting the Standard _____ 135

VI
RETIREMENT _____ 157

Celebrations Leading to my Retirement _____ 159
The Program _____ 162
My Retirement Speech _____ 163

VII
POST RETIREMENT_____ 169

Since Then _____ 171
Notes on Being Retired _____ 173
Fifty Things I Miss About Teaching _____ 175
What I Couldn't Say in the Classroom But Now Can _____ 179
The "Who"_____ 182
In Closing _____ 185

FOREWORD

I met Linda in 1982 when I joined the faculty of North Mesquite High School. Since that time she has not only been my colleague, but she has been my advisor and my dear friend. I always appreciated her talent as a teacher, but I never really understood the magnitude of her abilities until my daughter was in her program. Helping chaperone the trips that her Renaissance classes took each year was a special privilege that I will always treasure. What adventures we shared on those trips! Reading Linda's book reminds me once again of the special contributions she has made to the education of young people.

Her book also reminds me of why she is my good friend. Linda is the epitome of integrity, and she can be trusted implicitly. I trust her to listen to situations and to advise me with wisdom that comes from her heart as well as her head. Her generosity is legendary. She is generous with material things as well as with her love and understanding. She looks for the good in every person she meets, and she looks for the positive in every situation that comes her way.

Anyone who enjoys these qualities in a good friend will enjoy reading this book. It is Linda at her best.

—Gay Bennett, Friend

When I entered Mrs. Muhl's classroom at 15 years old, "the world" seemed to pose only a small challenge. Hardened, I had just emerged from the rubble of an emotional landslide; therefore, the nature of my self—more than anything about life "out there"—stumped me.

During Mrs. Muhl's Gifted and Talented Humanities class, I began thinking critically, asking hard questions of famous texts and crafting solid arguments in writing. From the class I made several friends, had opportunities to attend lectures and performances at a university in Dallas, and even traveled to New York for a week of Broadway with her.

However, from the stories "Mama" Muhl shared, I learned much more than language arts; I learned to live as a woman-child of integrity, leaving no experience—pleasurable or painful—untapped. When she begged me to search for meaning, I started to find *why* and *how* and for *whom* I do things rather than in the fleeting prestige of just "what I'm doing these days." I began an ongoing struggle to accept my own strengths and weaknesses so that I might move beyond self obsession to a life of service. When helpless and easy self pity seemed attractive, she coached that *I* could choose and create joy for myself—even when others did not accept it as an option. By inspiring me to serve and awakening me to the knowledge of choice, the wisdom of Mrs. Muhl saved me from a despair that once—and more than once— seemed too large to conquer. The beauty of being alive passes quickly, and the charms of lofty titles easily fade, but the freedom that comes from the truth in Mrs. Muhl's lessons will last much longer. Because of her influence, I have been able to live with the face staring back at me from my own mirror each night. I trust that after reading Mrs. Muhl's words and teachings, you will benefit likewise.

—Emily Southerland, Former Student

Mrs. Muhl's students will remember her forever. She taught them not only about literature and symbolism, but about life and their place in it. The responsibilities, the requirements, the expectations, the goals, the enjoyment, the appreciation, and the discipline that they learned from her will carry them through life, equipping them for the inevitable challenges ahead.

My own favorite teacher in Jacksonville, Texas, June Burns, taught me that education is not about memorizing facts, but about the process of learning and how we go about it. She posed more questions than she gave answers.

How does knowing something affect my life? Why do other people think differently than I? What difference does family and culture make in my perspective of the world? Why are my beliefs important? How do my beliefs mold me as a person? How willing would I be to change my belief system if challenged with new ideas or facts? These were lofty and difficult concerns for me, a teenager in East Texas, and often they made me uncomfortable. I was challenged and changed, and that was exactly her goal.

Mrs. Muhl has taught thousands of students who feel the same way about her. I know that many of her former students, including my own two, stay in touch with her on a regular basis. I am confident that those whom she has taught think of her regularly, pray for her, and thank God that He allowed them to walk in her shadow for a few years of high school. She is their June Burns.

As parents, my wife and I are so thankful for our own association with Mrs. Muhl. She always kept us informed about what was going on in her program. We trusted her completely, knowing that she always made teaching our children her first priority. We respect her for her fair treatment, her patience, and her love for not only our son and daughter, but for every student she ever taught.

For anyone who has had a June Burns or a Linda Muhl in his life, this is a must read!

—Doug Hall, Parent of Former Students

PREFACE

I never intended to write a book. In fact, I really had never thought I was author material. Even when people who found out I was retiring asked me the question, "Are you going to write a book when you retire?" my answer was always, "I don't think so. What on Earth would I write about?" Yet, here it is, my first and probably the only book I will ever pen.

I am sure that this book will not be something everyone will enjoy reading. It certainly will not have a universal audience; however, I do believe there are some who will want to go down Memory Lane with me. That is what this book is, an account of my life before, during, and after my career as a public school classroom teacher.

This "needing to remember" is what convinced me to write. I have loved my life, every minute of it. Even the hard times I have experienced, though hard to endure at times, are a part of who I am today, so I do not want to forget those challenges. Of course, I want to remember all the great experiences as well. Every person who has crossed my path—every family member, every friend, every co-worker, every parent, and every student I have taught— have influenced my life in some way, and I do not want to forget any of these remarkable people who have touched my life.

Because I realize that my memory is not what it once was, I decided that if I did not write everything down now while my "thinking" is still pretty good, I might just forget a part of all that has happened in my life. And I do not want to forget even one minute.

I sincerely hope that if you take the time to read my book, you will smile a little. Every time I reread it, I smile and sometimes shed a tear or two. I have had a good life, an exciting life, a busy life, thanks to many of you. Enjoy.

I

JUST ME

"A Dream Deferred"

On July 5, 1937, the last of Bryan and Odia Thompson's five children was born. This fourth daughter and fifth child was I, Linda Jo. My sisters tell of being called out of the field (where they were hoeing cotton) to see their little sister for the first time. My mother had all of her children at home, and although there was a doctor attending the birth, childbirth was never easy for her. Being the baby, I was always very close to my mother, and I still miss her even though she died at age 61, just a week before my daughter Sally was born.

I remember only snippets of my first five years in Aquilla, Texas. Actually my birth certificate shows Abbott, Texas, as the address, and my husband has always teased me about being born in the same town as Willy Nelson. I remember that we lived with my paternal grandparents who lived across the street from an open tabernacle, and my friends and I played there many a day, digging in the sand for doodlebugs, of all things!

In May of 1942, the trailer was packed in advance, and immediately after my sister Esteen graduated from high school, we moved to Mesquite. I was five at the time, and in September of that year, I began my school days at Mesquite Elementary School. Maynelle and Bryan, Jr., my other siblings, also graduated from Aquilla, but sister Nan and I graduated from Mesquite High School. In fact, the elementary, junior high, and high school were all on the same campus where just the high school sits now. Not until after I graduated did Florence Black Elementary open, Mesquite's first school separate from the main campus. Florence Black taught me American history and civics (what is now called government). Later, the first junior high opened, Agnew Junior High, named after my Algebra and Geometry teacher, Frank B. Agnew. During my school days, I also had as teachers Mary Moss, J. C. Cannaday, and Cecil Beasley, all of whom have had schools named for them.

I graduated 9th in my class of about sixty students. This means I was in the top ten, but not the top 10 per cent. I had a busy social life, and I would be the first to admit that studying was not my thing. This is in spite of the fact that I belonged to a group that called itself a study club. (Actually, we played cards a whole lot more than we studied.) Most of our meetings were held at the Porter's house. Bill Porter was and still is a good friend of mine. After teaching and being a principal, he now works part time for the district, recruiting new teachers. He usually came by my room at least once a year, and I strongly suspect it was so that he could tell my students that I was his girlfriend in the second grade. Actually, all the girls liked Bill because his dad owned the local drugstore, and he gave his girlfriends great gifts. I remember getting a heart-shaped box of candy that year for Valentine's Day.

I was always a good English student, and I loved to read. I also loved history. But when I was in the upper elementary grades, I competed in Interscholastic League math. I still love simple mathematics and can add a column almost as fast as I can put the numbers in the computer. I disliked geometry, though, because I am lousy at memorizing.

From my early school days, I decided that I wanted to be a teacher. When I was learning to read and write, we had a Spanish live-in lady who helped my mother with the housekeeping duties and me. By this time, we owned a grocery store in what is now considered North Mesquite. So when I got home from school, because she had never attended school, I taught her everything I learned. Even before that, my sisters tell me that I was lining my dolls up in order to "teach" them and shaking my finger at them when they misbehaved.

One of my best friends was a year ahead of me in school, and when she left to attend North Texas State University in Denton, the plan was that I would join her the next year. I never made it. I attended Draughn's Business College and went to work immediately for a Dallas bank. Later I transferred to the First National Bank in Mesquite where I worked until after Kip and Sally, two of my children, were born. The next job I had was as an apartment manager for the Highland Village Apartments complex near the hospital in Mesquite. From there, I worked as manager of the group health insurance department at a large insurance brokerage firm, Total Insurance Planning Service (TIPS for short). When I told a friend I was working for TIPS, she thought I was working at some restaurant for gratuities.

In 1968, my marriage of thirteen years fell apart. Approximately two years later, in March of 1971, I married my true love and soul mate, Drew. Within a couple of years, we had adopted each other's children, and I was living the life of a full-time mother and housewife for the first time in my life. At this time, Drew's boys, Andy and Peter, were twelve and ten, and Kip and Sally, my two, were eight and five. After I got them all off to school, I spent my time in ways I had never had the opportunity to explore before. I learned how to bowl and joined a bowling league. I was a member and even served as president of a knitting club. There I learned how to crochet, as well as how to master cross-stitch and crewel embroidery. I did a lot of picking up and delivering children to school activities and sporting events during these early years of our new family, also. I read quite a bit, picking an author and reading everything I could find by that author. I took tole-painting lessons but ended up doing all my artwork on wooden items. I did mostly fruit and flower patterns, and I still have some of these items hanging on my kitchen walls. I baked many a loaf of homemade bread during this time from a starter given to me by Jackie Baird, a good friend and mother of a former student, Keri. Most of these things were done as a result of my deciding to "master" some of the Early American arts. One Christmas I actually did some sewing (if you can call it that) by making a whole wardrobe of fancy dress-up clothes for my granddaughter Maci. Later, I made two porcelain dolls for her and her sister Tori. Both the sewing and the doll making were struggles, and although I was pleased with the outcome, I vowed never to do those two activities again.

After a few years of all this "learning to do new things," I became a little bored. Drew, knowing I had this "passed over" dream of being a teacher, suggested that I enroll and attend Eastfield College while the children were in school. I did this and loved every minute of every class I ever took there. After taking almost everything they had to offer and accumulating approximately 100 hours and at Drew's urging, I moved on to the University of Texas at Dallas. Majoring in English with teaching fields of both English and history, I graduated with honors. Intending only to substitute, Drew knew, after seeing me do my student teaching at McDonald Middle School, that I loved every minute of being in front of a classroom, so he suggested that I apply for a full-time teaching position. By this time, the youngest of our children, Sally, was a sophomore, so I had much less to do at the house. I was hired to teach American and World History at North Mesquite High School in 1979, on the day before school started. (I have always bragged about not having to go through new teacher training, but secretly, I have always felt cheated.)

It didn't take but a few weeks for me to realize that not only had I realized my dream, but I had also found my calling. Teaching had to be what God had in mind for me from the very beginning. To this day, I hate that my dream was deferred, but I have to acknowledge that since God was in charge, there had to be a good reason.

After my first year at North Mesquite, because I was "low man on the totem pole," I had to transfer to Wilkinson Middle School where I taught English and Texas history. At mid-term, in compliance with his promise, principal Bud Campbell called me back to North Mesquite to fill a pregnant teacher's English position. During my almost twenty years there, I taught English I; CLA English I; English II; English III; Honors English I; GT English I, II, and III; American History, World History, Advanced Texas Studies, and Mentorship.

While teaching at North Mesquite, I got my masters in—would you believe?—business and human development. I also received certification to teach gifted education at all levels during this time, which led to my being qualified to teach Gifted and Talented English once it was mandated for high school. Of course, I had to apply for this job, and I remember really "sweating it out" prior to the announcement that I had been selected.

When Dr. John D. Horn High School opened, I decided to follow my previous principal, Ronnie Pardun, to the new campus in order to get the GT English program set up as I had done previously at North. That first year, I also taught English I regular and English I honor students. There were only about 600 freshman and sophomore students that first year, so having three preparations was not unusual for every teacher. The next year, however, I was able to move to all GT classes which I taught until I retired in 2008.

I have always said that I am a result of the sum of my experience; therefore, I would not change a single thing about my life. Although a failed marriage is not something I am proud of, I am very blessed to have my son and daughter born of that marriage. I guess there had to be at least one "blip" in an otherwise wonderful life. How can I possibly complain? My dream may have been like the title of Langston Hughes' poem, "A Dream Deferred," but finally it was realized. I knew from the beginning that teaching was not only my dream; it was what God intended for my life.

My Work Ethic

Once I started working, I seldom ever missed a day of work. I suppose it started when my mother never let me give her lame excuses for not going to school. Actually, the truth is that school was such a social thing for me, I felt as if I would miss something if I did not attend every day. For several of my twelve years, I had perfect attendance. This record extended to my days as a soda jerk, a bank employee, an apartment manager, and an insurance manager.

I can almost tell you every day I missed once I began my teaching career. Seldom was an absence due to illness. Once I slipped on the floor of my classroom at North Mesquite. Because I couldn't get up immediately, they called an ambulance, and I was taken out on a stretcher. The doctor confirmed that I had a mild concussion, and I did miss the rest of that day and the next. My students collected money and gave my friend, Gay Bennett, the instructions to buy as many flowers as she could buy with the money they collected. That was the biggest, most beautiful bouquet of flowers I have ever seen, including all the casket sprays I have seen at funerals. She still had money left, so she bought a gift certificate for dinner at the Olive Garden.

Another time I was absent was the time I had a skin carcinoma removed from my nose. This problem and a family funeral at the same time took me out a couple of days. When I returned with stitches and my nose bandaged, I don't think my students appreciated it when I insisted that they see the picture that the plastic surgeon took of the hole before he repaired it. It was as big around as a dime and went all the way down to the cartilage. It really took almost all of one side of my rather small nose, but Dr. Byron Brown did a great job of giving me a new nose.

I waited until school was out in May to agree to my doctor's advice to have an hysterectomy. It was a quick recovery, and I had the whole summer to convalesce, so most of my students never even knew of it.

A couple of years later, breast cancer "cooperated" when it waited to appear in my life in June. I had my surgery in July then recuperated in Hawaii with my two good friends Lynne Henson and Gay Bennett. My students might not have ever known about this either, but the surgery was only the first step. Chemotherapy and radiation treatments began in August and were a challenge once school started; however, I managed to schedule all of my appointments after my classes so that I did not have to miss a single day of school for my treatment. I did try to make the best of this bad time. Because it seemed to affect my students more than anything I had ever shared with them, I tried to assure them that death was not something I was afraid of, but that made it worse. We all had a good cry; then it was back to the books. I did try to show everyone my bald head, but it did not seem to put them at ease, and some even hid their eyes and refused to look. But wearing a different color wig on a regular basis, I kept them guessing what I would look like each day, and somehow, we made it through that year with more laughs than tears.

Family funerals caused me to miss a few days, but other than that and my few sick days, the rest of my absences were due to school business. I hated to miss a day of teaching worse than anything, so it took a lot (such as a doctor's orders for me to stay in) for me to make the decision to call for a substitute.

AN IDEAL LIFE

A long time ago, I decided that I would lead the good life. I declared that I would always be a happy person, secure in the love of my God, my family, and my friends. "Happy" to me meant and still means "having serene and lasting joy." I tried always to work hard, take advantage of opportunities that came my way, and make good decisions concerning my future. Have all my decisions been good ones? No. But one thing there is about me: I have never looked back. Instead, I have moved forward, applying the lessons learned from my mistakes and making better decisions from that point forward. For instance, even though I aborted my plans to attend college right after high school (a bad decision), I eventually entered as a freshman at age thirty-six and reached my goal of becoming a teacher at age forty-two (one of the best decisions of my life).

My second marriage merged two families. My husband, Drew, had two boys, Andy and Peter, who were 12 and 10 at that time. I had a boy, Kip, who was 8, and a girl,

Sally, who was 5. We were fortunate in that we both ended up being able to adopt each other's children, giving us a family of 6. My new life with Drew was not without problems, for it is difficult to change one's circumstances over night. Yet, that is exactly what happened. I went from being employed in the work force (I had worked since before I was 16), to being a full-time housewife and mother; from being a mother of two children, to being a mother of four; from being a part of a Baptist congregation, to worshipping as a Presbyterian. Those first years were tough, but with perseverance, I finally got the children reared, held on to my marriage to a wonderful guy, and got my degree to enter the teaching profession.

There have been other threats to my happiness: the deaths of several family members, skin cancer on my nose that required plastic surgery, breast cancer (which is what caused the death of my mother), and the consequences of that cancer: chemotherapy, radiation, and hair loss. Yet, through all these calamities (and others), I have maintained that "serene and lasting joy" I willed myself from an early age.

Part of that "joy" comes as a result of the people who have been and are now in my life. I have been so fortunate to have such a wonderful family. Even though Drew and I love our children greatly, we are currently experiencing truly unconditional love for our ten grandchildren and two great-grandchildren. My family is one that has never experienced division in any way. Once my sister Nan's nemesis (we are six years apart), I am now her best friend and vise versa. We are so much alike that even we can see the resemblance in our looks and mannerisms. We think so much alike that we often read each other's mind or buy the same things. And since my retirement, I have gotten really close to my sisters Maynelle (soon to be 85) and Esteen (soon to be 83). I have also had a close relationship with my bother Bryan's family, and still do even though they are in Oregon and he is now deceased.

While I do not see many of my childhood friends very often, I still cherish my memories of time spent with them. Currently, my good friends and soul sisters, Gay Bennett and Lynne Henson, support me through my bad times and create many of my good times. We lunch together often, travel together when we can, and talk to each other ever chance we get. My Party Pals, what I call the group of about fifteen who party with me several times a year, are a special mix of kindred spirits that I thank God for on a regular basis.

And not to be slighted, the many wonderful young people I have been fortunate enough to teach over my twenty-eight-year career have had a tremendous impact on my "joy." Even though I may have had more interactions with some than others, I have never loved a single one of my students more than the others. Each one has had such an individualized impression on me that there is no way I could have chosen favorites. One of the best things that I realized about my gifted students is that by the third year as my student, each was convinced that he or she was my favorite. This is exactly what I always wanted them to believe, for every one of them is truly a part of who I am today.

Even though I have been a Christian since thirteen, and even though I have felt His strength and love in all my times of past troubles, it has only been lately that I have realized just how important He is in my life. I need Him more now than I have ever needed Him. I need Him to help me adjust to my life without teaching. I need Him to help me adjust to an aging body and ebbing energy. In other words, I need Him to help me to adjust to a less-than-perfect existence here on Earth. Most of my life, I have been much more focused on me than on others. If asked, I would have always said, "My life has been almost perfect; I get to be around the people I love, work at the ideal-for-me job, and experience lots of good times. But now, God is reminding me that life is not all about "me." So, in spite of my many benevolent community activities and occasional contributions to good causes, I see that God has finally given me a task that has the potential of earning me "stars in my crown": the task of taking care of my beloved husband Drew, who is slowly becoming a victim of dementia. This is not easy now and will get harder as time goes on. With prayer, mine and others', and with the support of friends and other family members, I will prove to God that I deserve his love and sacrifice.

So this is how I define and lay claim to "serene and lasting joy." With God, my family, my friends, and my students, any distractions will be merely blips on the screen, and happiness for me will be the everlasting picture throughout the rest of my time on Earth..

MY FAVORITE THINGS

This is really a hard topic to cover, but I will attempt to list some of my favorite things, in no particular order.

Eating Good food. I have always loved good food, probably because my mother was such a great cook. To eat at her table was a real privilege, not only because the food tasted so good, but because it was so beautifully prepared. My mother always cooked my favorite meal for my birthday: fried chicken, mashed potatoes and cream gravy, spinach, and homegrown sliced tomatoes. Her desserts always looked as if they came right off the pages of a cookbook, and her chocolate cake was to die for. For the first few years of my life, my mother and father lived on a farm where we raised our own meat sources and vegetables. Then, when I was about six, they bought a grocery store, so our family always had plenty of good food available. All of us daughters love to cook, and each of us, at some time, has published her own cookbook. I am bad about finding something that tastes really good to me and eating it over and over until I finally tire of it. Breakfast is my least favorite meal, but I always eat something. My first choice is a bacon and tomato sandwich with a diet coke, but I try not to eat this too often. Vegetables are tastier to me than meat, but that hasn't always been the case. I previously thought I had to have chicken, steak, pork chops, ribs, roast, or ham at every meal. Now, I enjoy a vegetable plate at times. I go for months liking lemon desserts best; then I will switch to apple or raspberry. Chocolate has to be my most consistent favorite, however. Mexican food is on the menu for me at least once or twice a month, but I love Chinese food and Italian food, too. Diet Coke is my soft drink choice, but iced tea is my favorite drink. I dislike water.

Reading a book that someone refers to me. I have always loved for a student or past student to say to me, "Oh, Mrs. Muhl, you have to read this book. " In fact, if anyone I know tells me to read a particular book, I really get excited about reading it. It is a two-pronged proposition: for one thing, I think it must be a good one in order for him or her to recommend it to me, and two, I am curious to see if I can determine why he or she thinks I would like it. I also love that, having read it, we (the recommender and I) now have something new to talk about.

Hosting family get-togethers. Whether it is all of them together or a few at a time, Drew and I really enjoy visits with our family members. When our children, all grown now, get together, there is a lot of reminiscing about the old days, and I never tire of hearing these stories. Invariably, someone will confess to something that happened years ago that is news to our ears. Of course, sometimes they tell us things that we already knew. We usually chose to pick our battles with our children, so sometimes we might let a "no-no" slide, leaving them to think they had gotten away with something, when in actuality, that was not the case. I really enjoy our grandchildren these days, but they are all growing up so fast that soon it will be hard to call them "children." It is also hard for them to find time to visit us because they all lead such active lives. I truly wish that we lived closer to all of them so that I could see them more often.

Having good friends. I have truly been blessed with good friends throughout my life. I had wonderful pre-school playmates, great school buddies, super couple friends, and some great adult friends, both men and women, who have gotten me through both good and bad times in my life. I have been extremely fortunate to add many of my students' parents to my list of friends, and even though none of their children are my students anymore, many of us are still in touch. Also, it is amazing how many of my past students are now my adult friends. I still communicate with many of them, and I will always be interested in where they are and in what they are doing in life. They seem to care for me in the same way. For a good portion of my adult life, I have enjoyed a wonderful relationship with my two soul mates, Gay Bennett and Lynne Henson. We have traveled together, vacationed together, partied together, laughed together, and cried together more times than I could ever mention. For years I have heard that "Two is company; three's a crowd," but we three have the perfect relationship. We each have roles; therefore, there is no competition among us. We take care of one another, and together, we make decisions that are good for all of us. We can almost read each other's minds because we have been friends for so long. In addition to being my cousin, Janene Nations is also a good friend. She and her husband, James, were our best couple friends for years. Even though James is no longer with us, we still see Janene almost weekly, and we talk on the phone every few days. My sister Nan is more than just my sister; she is also my friend. We are very much alike in so many ways, and we have never had a secret from each other in our entire lives. We talk almost daily even though she lives in Mississippi, and we visit each other at least three or four times a year. Lately, I have been a member of a group called The Who, Women Helping Others. This group of fifteen women are wonderful people who care about others to the point that they actively do something about it. It is such a privilege to be a part of this group, and I count every one of them my good friends because we are so united in purpose. We make one another laugh and have a great time whenever we are together.

Going to church. I haven't always felt this way. Going

to church, for many years, was more a ritual or a responsibility than something I loved to do. Now that I am a member of C Life Church of Forney, I love going. I love seeing so many of my past students and their parents, and I really like that one of my past students from North Mesquite, Casey Coats, is on staff there. In fact, I can hardly wait to hear the sermon because it is always so relevant to my life and where I am now. My sister feels the same way about her church, so often we find ourselves re-preaching our sermons to each other on Sunday afternoons. I have to admit that I have had to get used to the "modern Christian rock" music at this church, but because I have always loved young people, these young musicians have now won my heart. I look forward to one day being able to "jam" with the best of them, but right now, I am mostly lip-synching.

Going shopping. I have shopped all my life but not always for myself. In fact, my favorite shopping is for others. I think I must have been a personal shopper in another life (ha, ha) because I have always shopped for people I know well, particularly those who, themselves, hate to shop. My daughter always hated to shop, so most all of her clothes were bought and brought home to her, even when she was in high school and college. I could please her more than she could ever please herself, back then. In fact, if she did go alone and make a purchase, she would often say to me, "Mother, would you take this back and see if you can find something I would like better?" I like to go with others to shop and find things for them that they are looking for. I usually find too much and a decision has to be made: "Which should I buy?" My reply is usually, "Buy them all."

Teaching. I know how unusual it is for someone to find one's "job" synonymous with "one of his/her favorite things," but that is just what teaching always was and always will be for me. The reason is that it was so much more than just a job. I was just born to teach. It was my calling, and I still think there are a few miles left in me. God has yet to reveal when, where, and how, but I feel confident that there is still a little more teaching left in me. In other words, it is still one of my favorite things to do.

I guess you can see that this is more than a list of my favorite things. These paragraphs say a lot about who I am and where I am in life. Some of my "favorites" have and/or will change as life goes on, but some will remain on my favorite list forever. So, in a way, this list also tells you about some of my values.

II

DECISIONS,
DECISIONS

To Substitute or Not?

When I graduated in December of 1978 from University of Texas at Dallas, I still thought I would probably just be a substitute teacher. Since I would not have been able to get a full-time job until the next school year, I realized I had a semester to see if I really wanted to become a substitute teacher instead of a full-time teacher. There were certainly benefits, namely being able to say "no" when called to substitute, if there was something else I needed to do, not to mention limited grading (if any). I first limited myself to substituting at any level of an MISD school. I quickly decided, however, that elementary school assignments were not for me. Getting little people to stay in their seats was almost impossible, peeling them off me was a hassle, and getting them lined up to go to lunch and to go "potty" was a real challenge. From then on, I limited myself to middle and high schools only.

At this time, two of my children, son Kip and daughter Sally, still attended North Mesquite. Although Sally did not mind my being there, Kip was afraid that I would run into him and make a scene. I had to promise to look the other way if I happened to pass him in the hall. I really enjoyed substituting there, however, and did so every time the principal called me.

The last six weeks of that semester, I was called to finish out the year for a special education teacher at West Mesquite High School. I taught these students very practical things, such as how to alphabetize, and I thoroughly enjoyed teaching these unique young people. At that time, Mrs. Janecka, the cafeteria manager, would often make kolaches that were to die for. I probably gained ten pounds during that six weeks.

Just before I took the permanent substituting job at West Mesquite High, I called Forney Independent Schools and substituted for them about three times before I took my name out of the hat. Forney High School is the school responsible for my most memorable substituting experience. One morning I was in the teachers' lounge, waiting to go to my assignment, when a group of young coaches asked me whose classes I was there to teach. After telling them, they advised me that after lunch, I was going to be exposed to a "class from hell." I thanked them and then asked if they had any pointers for me. One young coach told me that one of his freshman football players was probably one of the ring leaders, so if I needed to reprimand him, just to threaten to get the coaching staff involved. All morning I plotted my course of action. When the bell rang after lunch, I tried to get students to sit down and listen to me. I could tell that this class was living up to expectations. They ignored me. I then called on Jeff Dewberry, the freshman football player, to step outside the room. He was immediately all puffed up, wondering what I wanted with him and hesitant even to follow my edict. I told him that I had heard from several people on campus that he was a real leader and that if I needed any help with this "wild" class, he would be the one to help me. I explained that if I could not get their attention, I would not be able to earn my salary by teaching what the teacher had left for me to teach. I watched his face change from disdain to a half smile. He asked me the names of those who told me of his leadership, and without giving him that answer, I again pressed for his help. He agreed, and I was immediately hopeful. Once inside the room, these words came out of his mouth: "Sit down, shut up, and listen to what this lady has to say." I am telling you the truth when I say that from that point on, I had their attention. I have never forgotten this experience, and many times when before a group of new teachers or when I have been a guest speaker at my daughter-in-law's college class of Introduction to Education, I have shared this story. I have to say that this incident was the beginning of my success with discipline in the classroom. Throughout my twenty-eight years of teaching, I never had a discipline problem that I did not solve immediately.

But this is not the end of that story. On July 7, 2009, I walked into Horn High School. I had not been there much since retiring (too painful), and when the security guards standing in the hallway saw me enter, they all spoke, and one said, "Mrs. Muhl, it's so good to see you." I noticed a young man in an MISD uniform about to leave the premises. He stopped in his tracks and asked me, "Are you really Mrs. Muhl? I knew a Mrs. Muhl thirty years ago, and I've never heard that name since." He asked me if I had ever subbed at Forney High School, and at that time, I knew exactly with whom I was speaking. Here he was again in my life, Jeff Dewberry. He told me that in that short period, I had made a difference in his life; therefore, he had not forgotten and would never forget me. Believe me, I will never forget him!

MIDDLE OR HIGH? THAT WAS THE QUESTION

I did my student teaching at McDonald Middle School. Since I was certified to teach English and history 7-12, I was placed where there was a need. The seventh grade English and speech teacher had requested a student teacher, and I was chosen by the district to fill the request.

Since my children had all attended McDonald, I was thrilled to work where I knew so many of the teachers. They were all extremely helpful, in particular the principal, Wayne Shamblin, and another then English teacher, Cindy Smethie. They were the main reasons why I received an A for Student Teaching. Ironically, I became the main teacher for the last few weeks when the supervising teacher, who was pregnant, had her baby prematurely. I taught Ms. Boudreau's speech class, also, even though I was not certified to teach speech. A speech class Reader's Theatre presentation to other classes was the highlight of that experience. Because of all the spelling lessons that had to be taught in the English classes, I learned and memorized the main spelling rules for the first time. This exposure to spelling would come in handy for the rest of my life, both personally and professionally. I got very attached to these first students even though I had them for only a short while, and after my graduation the next December, I loved getting calls to substitute there.

Even though I enjoyed my stay at McDonald, because I most enjoyed all my substituting at the high school, I pretty much decided that if I decided to teach full time, I would pursue teaching at the high school level. I did not decide to apply for a full-time position until after school began in 1979. Fortunately, a basketball coach, Coach Brooks, resigned the day before school started, and I was hired to teach his American and World History classes at North Mesquite High School. I just knew I was the most fortunate person alive at this point, but I have always regretted never getting to attend new teacher in-service. That training and exposure was already over, and school started the very next day after I was hired. In my World History classes were many of my daughter Sally's friends. It was a good thing that she learned early to say, "That's your problem, not mine," when one of them complained about how hard I was. I really enjoyed teaching them, though, because I knew so many of them and because they were really a sharp group of students. We did many creative projects in both history classes. I specifically remember one student making a television out of a huge cardboard box in order to present her oral report "live." I even invited a WWII veteran, Robert Lee Hanby, to come speak to them about his war experiences.

The very next year, North Mesquite had two hundred fewer students; therefore, several teachers had to go. Because I was the last one hired, my fate was sealed. Mr. Bud Campbell, the then principal, told me that if I would go to Wilkinson Middle School to teach English and Texas history, he would see that I could come back to NM the next year. I really enjoyed teaching at Wilkinson and was really feeling a sense of accomplishment by getting students ready for high school, when I was transferred back to North Mesquite at mid-term. Ruth Copeland, who taught freshman and sophomore English, was taking a maternity leave, and I stepped right into her classes, cold turkey. I loved everything about this assignment but climbing to the top floor, the English floor. It was only a couple of years later that I became cheerleader sponsor and was moved to ground level rooms from then to the end of my days at North Mesquite.

So, as "fate" would have it, I became a high school teacher. It could have gone either way. There were times in my high school career that I wished I could teach seventh graders. That is where all the final basic instruction happens, and I felt that I could give students that firm foundation they would need for high school and college. Because the rest of the public school years focus on further development of the basics, I believed (and still do) that seventh grade is the most critical year for English instruction.

Of course, the more I taught, the more I knew that it really wasn't fate at all; God's purpose for my life really began when I entered the doors of North Mesquite and Horn. My teaching experiences at both high schools could not have been better. I knew when I walked out of Horn's door for the final time that I had done the right thing all along. Teaching—teaching at the high school level—was definitely my "calling."

III

UNEXPECTED PERKS

LIFE-LONG LEARNING 1

The school district that I worked for my whole career, Mesquite ISD, had one particular superintendent, Dr. John Horn, who focused on promoting life-long learning. I interpreted this in a very personal way: I felt that I had to excite students about learning while in school so that they would carry this love for learning throughout their lives. I personally am a "learner." I am always looking for a challenge, and I have learned that one sure way for me to be challenged is to become occupied with learning to do something that I have never done before.

One particular summer I decided to master the early American arts. I learned how to crochet, how to embroidery, how to make homemade bread and preserves, and how to latch hook a rug. A later summer, I decided I would learn how to create porcelain dolls so that I could recreate the images of my small granddaughters. Still another summer, my challenge was making "dress-up" clothes for my then 5-year-old granddaughter. I have to admit that although I reached an acceptable level of competency which I always require of myself, some of these skills have since been put to bed. Doll-making, for instance, was just a too tedious and painstaking job for my comfort. If I remember correctly, I had to replace one head, one arm and one leg before I finally got the first one put together. Porcelain is so delicate!

Because I have experienced so many good feelings from having learned new things all my life, one of my objectives in the classroom was to get students excited about learning. Sometimes it was to give them just a little taste of pleasure they could expect from learning more. Sometimes it was to require their participation in a new project, hoping that their creativity would kick in and increase the enjoyment that lay in store for them. I am not sure how successful I was at accomplishing this objective, however. I think perhaps this success has to be measured in retrospect, long after students leave high school.

LIFE-LONG LEARNING 2

About five years ago, I stumbled on an article about life-long learning that is another way of looking at the term. A teacher spoke of remembering how his own three children always answered the proverbial question, "What did you learn in school today?" Of course, they answered him the same way that millions of school children have answered their parents who asked that same question: "Nothing." This made him wonder just how memorable his own lessons were and how his students would answer this question if someone asked it of them as they exited his classroom.

Reading about his experience made me wonder the same thing and brought me to a new way of teaching my students. One of my teachers in junior high school once told us students that the brain is nothing more than a filing system for remembering what we learn and/or experience in life. So I started thinking that if teachers taught by first setting up a file in their students' brains, then all the information shared about that same subject could be permanently stored in that file. Now, this would truly be "life-long learning"! I decided that to set up a file on everything I taught, I had to give my students a label for each lesson. I knew that up front, I would have to make sure I gave my objective, from which they could derive a label. For instance, if I were going to teach the skills of good leadership, I would have to make sure that I told them the objective up front, not just start in on the lesson. To further make sure the label worked, I would have to reiterate the rationale for learning this information and what the benefits would be if it were mastered, throughout the entire lesson. Even after the lesson was over, any time I ran across more material on good leadership, the students could file it with their other information—all for future use as needed. It would be interesting to me to see just how much my students remember about leadership training, or for that matter, anything else that I taught them. I guess maybe I will never know. . .

Sharing Talents

I don't know when I first heard the Bible story about talents found in the 19th chapter of Matthew. What I do know is that I have always believed that if a person who is gifted does not share his talents, he will lose them.

When I first started teaching English at North Mesquite High School, I would often ask my fellow teachers for ideas. I often got lame excuses: "I don't have anything you would really want." or "I'll try to find something, but I mostly just do what the textbook says do." The real truth is that many teachers were and are very territorial about their materials. Even if they had good ideas, they wanted to keep them for themselves. I never understood this because we were all English teachers, and none of us would teach the same students on a given level. To get help, I finally called on two of my friends who happened to be teaching English at West Mesquite: Judy Heaps and Esta Ann Hart. They came over one day after school with an armload of ideas that finally got me off to a good start. I decided then that I would never be selfish with any good idea I might have. Over the course of my twenty-eight years, I have conducted in-service for teachers of the Mesquite school district, the Terrell school district, the Sunnyvale school district, and several others. I have also conducted workshops for Region 10, for the Texas Gifted and Talented Association, and for any other entity that asked for my services. I believe that I have a talent for teaching. That fact is the reason I have always shared my ideas. I love teaching too much to have it taken away. Perhaps it is this message from God that has caused me to look continually for new ways to "teach." By the same token, I have always felt the need to continue honing my talent. Who knows when and where I will again be called to teach? There are so many societal changes occurring, that one must be on his/her toes to make necessary adjustments.

I often had trouble convincing my students to share their talents. There was nothing I enjoyed more than to see my students perform. Whether that was playing a sport, performing in the area of the fine arts, or just participating in class, I loved watching them excel. But some were shy about performing in front of others. Some were even shy about contributing in class even when they had done the assignment and were prepared to participate optimally. One of the reasons behind my tables-around-the-room classroom arrangement is so that I could help them develop confidence. Many students, over the years, commented that my class helped them feel better about performing in front of others.

The fact that every time they opened their mouths they were in front of the group had to have helped them.

When I retired, it thrilled me that so many of my past and present students performed at my retirement ceremony. Whether they sang, recited, played, or presented, they thrilled me to my core. There are so many times that I have dreamed that my funeral lasted for a whole day because there were so many of my past students who wanted to perform or speak. I guess this has occurred in my subconscious because nothing would bring me more pleasure.

Happiness, Better Known as "Supreme and Lasting Joy"

When I began teaching, I saw such angst in some of my students that I decided I should try to incorporate a lesson on "how to be happy." Shortly into my preparation, I realized that happiness cannot be taught. In took a while for me to feel good about approaching the subject of happiness in the classroom.

The History of Rasselas, Prince of Abyssinia, is a book that I began having my gifted students read. It is a college-level text, but it has a great message concerning happiness. The focus of the story is Rasselas' search for happiness. He escapes his confinement, yet he ultimately realizes that one cannot "search for and find" happiness; he must create it for himself. He returns from his futile search in order to continue his training to be a good ruler to his people. He, like many of us, realizes that doing a good job at what one is called to do is one way to create happiness for oneself.

I certainly considered the profession of teaching my

"calling." I felt like this is exactly what God had given me as my purpose in life. It was so much more than an occupation or profession. Of course, it took me a long time to realize this. I went to business college right after high school and promptly went to work at a bank. After nine years and several promotions, I left banking to become the manager of the first large apartment complex in Mesquite, Highland Village Apartments. After that, I became the group health department manager at an insurance brokerage firm in North Dallas, owned by a Mesquite friend. It was after a second marriage to a husband who allowed me to follow my dream of getting a college degree, that I finally became the teacher I was intended to be. At age 42, I finally became a public school teacher. So you see, my search took quite a while. I loved every job I ever had, and I experienced much happiness and some unhappiness prior to becoming a teacher, but it took being a teacher for me to get to the stage that I call "supreme and lasting joy." I was fulfilling God's purpose for my life.

The "happiness" that I always referenced in my lessons is really better described as "life-long joy." It transcends the "downs" and the "sad times" that we all have to go through as a part of life. We erroneously describe the "ups" in our lives as happiness, but "true-and-lasting-joy happiness" comes only after we find our niche in life, in tune with God's purpose for us. I truly believe that we all have access to this purpose. Some people get to serve that purpose within their professions or jobs. Others have to reach that satisfaction after work hours.

I once knew a man who as a young man loved three things: playing in a band, researching war planes, and studying biology. He decided that he could go to college to become a doctor then use the medical profession to finance his love for restoring war planes. On the side, he formed a band among his friends and performed on weekends to satisfy his love of music. After a close self-analysis, he found a way to experience "true and lasting joy." He was doing several things he loved to do, something he felt he was "called" to do, and serving others in the process. With many students talented in the performing arts, I often heard them express a desire to perform on stage. Most of us know how few actually can make a living in the performance arena; however, I always told them that a paying profession does not have to take away from that joy one gets by performing. I suggested that they pursue other interests in order to finance their true love for a particular performing art. That way, "true and lasting joy" could still be experienced.

Although I have not found an actual way to teach a person how to be happy, I have come up with some pretty strong ideas about how one can acquire it for himself. Here is my advice:

1. Probably the first and most important thing I believe is essential is that you pray about it. God will answer your prayers and lead you to make good decisions about your life.

2. Get to know yourself well, for only self-knowledge,

not what others think, is the key to "life-long joy."

3. Figure out a way to experience pleasure along with work, or find other work.

4. Find a way to feel good about what you do. This usually relates to "what's in it for those other than myself," which really helps define your purpose. It is also another way of serving God because as we do for others, we also do for our Lord.

5. While money is essential to existence, making lots of money should not be a goal **greater than** what it will take for you to experience "supreme and lasting joy."

Supporting Community Service

Once I became involved in teaching gifted and talented students, I realized that I had a special challenge. Having them for three years meant that I had to provide more than just information about my subject. If they were to grow and mature into responsible adults, I had to alert them to the responsibilities of good citizenship. I had to make them aware of the needs of the community that they, as young people, could serve.

People from the surrounding community were always asking me to give them names of students who could help with a specific cause. Some of these were associated with the Mesquite Public Library, the City of Mesquite, various North Mesquite elementary schools, and even merchants at the mall. Because I felt responsible, I decided to organize a club that would not only encourage my students to do community service but would keep up with individual hours. It was noteworthy that some colleges were expecting incoming freshmen to be service-minded, and some even used community service as a possible topic for college entrance essays. This meant that by forming a service club for my students, I was "killing several birds with one stone."

The RSVP before "Club" meant Renaissance Students' Volunteer Projects, and that is how it got started. I controlled the activities based on demand. If an elementary school principal asked for ten students who could tutor students in math, I felt comfortable getting ten students to volunteer. It was limited to my students only, and I filled only those requests that I felt my students could be good at doing.

Soon, every student at North Mesquite was asking to be included. At this time we actually started the RSVP Club. The projects were still Renaissance sponsored, the officers were all Renaissance students, and the sponsor was still I, the Renaissance teacher, but we had large meetings in the auditorium, encouraging all students on campus to volunteer. A system was established whereby students could keep up with their own hours. This worked well and continued until I left North Mesquite.

Once at Horn, I started the same club. We met monthly and published a newsletter telling of the volunteer opportunities that were available at the time. I also was part of establishing a community service program whereby a certain number of hours were required each of the four high school years. If a student met the requirements, he or she would then be presented a special award at graduation. This plan worked well until the founders could find no relievers. It is hard to get teachers to volunteer to do things outside their classrooms. Many have small children they need to get home to, and many such responsibilities require staying after school. Some even entail evening and weekend hours. I hated to see this project fizzle, but due to a lack of sponsorship, there was no remedy.

I do feel that I was blessed to be a part of such programs as these. Many of my students learned of the "warm" feelings one gets from serving others. I continued to support community service projects, but the last few years, they were within my own classes, utilizing only my students. We got really creative.

One year we had a food drive to help fill empty shelves at the Mesquite Social Services headquarters. Each student was to come up with his own way of collecting, and prizes were given to those who collected the most. One student who had a great voice went door to door, singing for those who agreed to contribute. Another known for her beautiful voice held a private concert for friends of the family, requiring food as admission. One called all his family members who were coming to a family birthday party, asking them to bring canned goods with them. Several set up donation boxes at fire stations and other businesses. Two girls partnered and pulled a little red wagon down neighborhood streets. We ended up collecting "tons" of food for this project.

Another impressive project started out meagerly but then grew to be the most successful of all. I brought a Christmas tree from home, and students brought their dollar bills to serve as the ornaments. This activity was to be our

Christmas project for the year, but at the end, we only had about $120., not a very impressive amount. So we decided to change from its being a Christmas project to a "double your dollars" spring project. Since everyone had brought a dollar for December, he or she would double the amount and bring $2.00 for January, $4.00 for February, $8.00 for March, and $16.00 for April. If everyone participated, it would net us over $3,000. Students were not to ask parents for any of this money. They were to baby-sit, rake leaves, or whatever it took to get it. The kids really had a great time doing the project, and in April, they voted on how to spend the money raised. They chose about five different organizations to split it among, and I was impressed when they decided to donate some of it to sponsor Emily Montana, one of my students, and her mother, Cynthia, who ran the 60 mile Race for Cancer Cure in my name.

Even though I am retired, I am still doing little community service projects. I have convinced my "party people" friends to join me in some of these projects. I guess all the "giving" lessons rubbed off on me because I am constantly thinking of new ways for my friends and me to help others.

PLAYING CUPID

Many teachers are very involved in their students' love lives. Ironically, even though my students came to me for many other personal reasons, they never came to me to talk about their romantic relationships. Unless I saw two of my students together with amorous looks for each other, I never knew who was dating whom. I always said that students didn't ask or tell me this information because my approval was always important to them, and what if I didn't approve? I'm sure this isn't correct, but I laughingly said it many times.

I did sort of play the role of cupid on occasion over the years. Sometimes on purpose, like the time I put Libby Thomas in the same group as her eventual husband, Terry Holley. It must have been a good match because they are still happily married and have a precious young daughter.

Another couple who became much better acquainted as a result of my class was not an intentional match on my part, but it has worked out well also. I was surprised at their attraction for each other at first, but I shouldn't have been; opposites do attract, or so the saying goes. Serious Jessica Bennett and laid-back Justin Wynne are now married and have two darling daughters.

I had nothing to do with another match between two of my students.. In fact, they are so obviously a match that they would have found each other even if they had not been introduced by a mutual friend when they were my students. They actually didn't start dating until their sophomore year in college. Amy Frith and Brandon Burriss are happily married and now have son, Will, to keep them even closer.

Eric Liga and Diana Moreno-Branum were an unexpected match, but their marriage is still in place, and they have at least one child.

Melissa Hennessey and Jordan Breeding were both in my class, and it was my Symposium assignment that first brought them together for in-depth discussion, which led to several years of dating. They are now husband and wife.

Another couple waited quite a while to tie the knot, but Chelsea Pierce and James Fox are now married, after having been together since their Muhl days at North Mesquite.

It took Marie Ibarra and Oliver Martinez even longer, but they are now (as of June, 2009) husband and wife, also.

I have had a few matches in mind over the years, but either one or both were not interested, or like the match I had in mind for Katie Davis and Christian Rodriguez, I waited too long. The day I called Katie to tell her my plan is the day she told me that she had just met her mate. She is living in Louisiana after getting married in August, 2009. Christian gets a kick out of my attempt at match-making, but someone has to do it for him. He is much too busy establishing a successful career in management. By the way, he is tall, dark, handsome, and smart, in case anyone is interested. I have to do something for him because he has promised that when my eyes no longer can see the words on a page, he will come read to me.

It is not surprising to me that many of my students dated over the years. My classes were always very loosely structured (except when I was teaching, of course), and many of my assignments called for group or partner hook-ups. And gifted students, in particular, have lots in common. These couples are the ones that I know about. There are still some Horn matches on the burner, but I will just have to wait to see if they lead to a permanent union.

A DOVE ON MY SHOULDER

I always tried to get my students to understand that when they could make allusions to literary classics or great paintings or important historical events or great music, or any other thing that is studied universally, they were proving to the world that they were well educated. In a sense, I tried to explain that these allusions are a universal language in and of themselves. People all over the world study many of the same classics as we do here in American, so even strangers who are schooled in the classics can have something to discuss.

I once had a student, Micah Pardun, who attended Austin College in Sherman. He returned home for his first visit, sharing with me that he had really impressed one of his professors with his writing, in particular by his use of allusions. This, and many other such testimonies, convinced me that I should try to expose my students to as many of the fine arts as possible. I wanted them to be able to converse with "the best of them," and I believed that knowledge of the classic arts would enhance that skill.

I also modeled the use of allusions on a regular basis. One of my most used allusions was a reference I would make to the Biblical account of Jesus' baptism. If you will remember, when Jesus was baptized, a dove landed on his shoulder, and the voice of God said, "This is my beloved Son in whom I am well pleased." I often felt the pleasure of thinking I was doing the right thing, and because it was such a perfect coincidence, I had to push it past "coincidence" and give God the credit for helping me with my job. For instance, on the weekend just before beginning a unit on leadership, I might find an article in the newspaper that was perfect for ushering in the new unit, and I was so pleased at my good fortune. To me, this was a sign that I must be doing the right thing at the right time; otherwise, how could this find be so perfect for my need? I would then tell my students, "This weekend I had a 'dove on my shoulder' experience. I just happened to find the perfect article for you to read before we begin our leadership unit."

There are now so many allusions that my students can understand and even use themselves. Certainly they know what kind of person a politician is when he is referred to as being Machiavellian, an allusion to *The Prince*. They can understand many allusions from our annual study of Shakespeare's great works, such as those that relate to the ides of March mentioned in *Julius Caesar*. They can understand many famous often-used sayings that relate to the ancient works of Homer, such as those that refer to the Trojan horse,

Achilles' heel, Helen's beauty, and many more. I sincerely hope my students continue to use allusions in their writing and in their conversations, but even if they do not, they should be able to understand when others do.

The real truth is that I sort of feel like my whole teaching experience was a "dove-on-my-shoulder" experience. I always felt that being in that high school classroom was exactly the place I should be. I felt that way from the beginning, all the way to the end. I never wanted to advance to administration, become a librarian or counselor, and I never wanted to teach at the college level. I felt like God had blessed me by giving me the opportunity (through Drew) to teach, so I needed to do the very best job possible. I also believe that he continually gave me signs that he was pleased with my work, particularly through conveniently having things come my way at just the right time.

BLEEDING GREEN

Green is definitely my favorite color. I wear lots of green clothes, and I have many green furnishings in my home. My favorite gem is an emerald, and even my eyes are green.

Green indicates renewal and growth, such as all the sprouts of spring that replace the death of winter. Green lights mean "go," pleasing those who are excited about making things happen.

A man once told me that green is the ideal color to use when you are trying to appeal to others. Why? Because, according to him, money is green, and everyone loves money!

The color red makes bulls angry. Blood is red, and many hate the sight of blood. Red ink indicates financial woes.

I am not sure what made me pick up that first green pen to do my grading, but that is what I did. Somehow, I felt that students would not feel as punished for their mistakes if I pointed them out in green instead of red, the traditional color of grading pens.

The goal of every student in my class was no more than I expected: by the time they were juniors, their papers should be free of green ink. This was a time of celebration for many of my students who reached "our" goal. Occasionally, there would be a sophomore who experienced the satisfaction of a paper with no green ink, but usually, it took three years of green corrections before all the "common errors" lessons were learned.

I suppose one would say that I became famous for my use of green pens. My students, however, definitely had conflicting emotions related to this choice of mine. It was not unusual, particularly at the start of each school year, for a student to whine, "My paper is bleeding green." While this might seem like a complaint, it is nothing compared to the complaints I would get when I did not have a green pen handy and wanted to do some grading. Once a student even asked me if I would go over my corrections in green ink. What is even more surprising is that even though they hated to see green marks on their returned papers, it was not uncommon for them to compare the number of such corrections, almost to brag about their own "green." Odd as it may seem, students actually got attached to the green that adorned their papers. I guess you might say that they had a love/hate relationship with my grading pen.

So early on, the green pen became a permanent tool of my trade. There is no way I could have ever changed colors. And why on Earth would I have wanted to?

LAUGHTER, THE BEST MEDICINE

One of the principles I tried to teach my students involved "saving face." I always told them a way to keep from being embarrassed when they did something or said something stupid in front of people: "You should always remember to start laughing immediately. This way, when others start laughing, they will be laughing <u>with</u> you and not <u>at</u> you."

I learned this lesson over the years because it was and is not uncommon for me to "stick my foot in my mouth." A couple of incidents that come to my mind happened when I worked at the First National Bank of Mesquite (back when there was such a thing).

While serving as a savings and loan teller back in the late 1950's, I had a man who always came to my window on Friday afternoon to get change for the machines at the washerteria where he did his weekly wash. For those of you who have never heard of washerterias, they were businesses that had wringer machines where people took their clothes to do their weekly wash. Very few had their own washing machines at this time, and wringer machines were a scale above having to use a wash board in the sink. One afternoon, in order to be cheery, I greeted him with, "Hello, sir. Are you here for your pickles and ninnies?" This was a far cry from the "nickels and pennies" I intended to say. My fellow teller, Margie Watson, never let me live this one down.

The second "most embarrassing moment" while working at the bank came after a customer, a slightly challenged young woman who ran the local snow cone stand, had come into the bank for a third time in one week to withdraw money from her savings account. As you know, these accounts are for deposits that are "saved," and I was irritated that she was using it as if it were a checking account. I marched into the office of the president of the bank, Gene Shands, and spouted, "This woman has entirely too many actions a week. Something has to be done." His reply was, "Milk of Magnesia? Imodium AD?" Years later I was still being teased. Oh, how I wished that I had used the word "transactions" instead of "actions."

Probably the most embarrassing moment of all times came after I had been teaching a while. At the end of one of the big fund-raising-for-New York garage sales at North Mesquite, someone suggested that we chaperons all go to On the Border for some cool refreshment and snacks. This was when we had our garage sales outside on the front yard of the school, and after yelling through the cheerleader megaphone for hours in the heat, I was the first to say, "Let's go." After being seated and served, the waiter asked if he could get us anything else, to which I replied: "I need some underwear." His smart retort was, "Lady, I don't think I can help you in that area." My tired mind and body just got "silver wear" and "underwear" mixed up, but my "so-called" good friends just couldn't let it go. Needless to say, I still have not lived this one down.

So, this is one principle of mine that I know works. I have had, and probably will still have, lots of opportunities to put it into practice. And why not? A good laugh at oneself is not only face-saving; it is very therapeutic.

IV

BASIC CURRICULUM

TEACHING VOCABULARY

I, personally, have always been a "word lover." Several times in my early adult life (prior to my teaching years), I would purchase a book such as *It Pays to Increase Your Vocabulary* and work my way through its lessons. Because I have always been a reader, I have a pretty good working vocabulary, or at least, my students always thought so. Knowing the meaning of a word and knowing how to pronounce it, however, are two different things. Many times over the years, I can remember knowing exactly what a word meant but embarrassing myself by mispronouncing it. One of these words is "pseudo." I can't remember how long ago I learned what a pseudo intellectual is, but it took embarrassment to teach me how to pronounce it. I realized the "p" was silent, but because it looked more like "suede" than "sued" to me, I pronounced it "seude-o" until someone called me on it. Like many of my students, I mispronounced "hyperbole" for a time after I knew what one was.

Before I leave the pitfalls of mispronunciation, I have

to teach one more time about how to pronounce last names. A person has the right to request a certain pronunciation of his last name, regardless of how it is pronounced by others who have the same last name. A perfect example, which I have always given, involves the two Presidents named Roosevelt. Even though they were distant cousins, Teddy emphasized the "oo" (which I remember by calling him "Teddy Roo"). Franklin chose to have his name pronounced as if it has one "o," like a "rose" (which I remember by calling him "Franklin Rose." I always demonstrated additional confirmation of this pronunciation rule by explaining that my husband's great grandfather dropped the "umlaut" when he came to America, changing the pronunciation of "Muhl" from "Muhl as in rule" (which is how his Old World ancestors pronounced it) to "Muhl as in mulberry" (which is how all the current Muhls pronounce it).

Another thing that I noticed in my years of teaching is that those students who took Latin could better decipher the meaning of a word they had never heard before because they had learned the meanings of Latin prefixes and suffixes that so many of our words have. To me, this was a tremendous benefit, and although I tried not to recommend generally a particular foreign language to my students, if they asked me my opinion, at that time and for this reason, I always suggested Latin.

Over the years I included vocabulary as a part of my curriculum even though I always have debated about whether studying vocabulary is a valid way to increase one's vocabulary. This is because I have always realized that people with the best vocabularies are those who are avid readers. This says that there is no better way to learn the meaning of words than to see them over and over in a variety of contexts. Context clues allow one to deduce, or at least to make a good guess, at what a given word means.

At times, however, I would attempt to "teach" vocabulary words. In my earlier years at North Mesquite, I remember assigning each student a different word to present to the class. From those lessons, I will never forget the meaning of "ebullient." One of my students, Rhonda Weeks, drew bubbles on the board, and I still remember that an "ebullient" person has a bubbly personality.

On every vocabulary test, I would give students varied contexts to prove to me that they knew the words. For instance, I might say, "Use the word 'machiavellian' in a sentence telling me about someone you know or know of." I would often have them tie the words to literature they were reading or had read, such as, "Use the word 'alienated' to describe any character from the book *Of Mice and Men*." Sometime I might have them write original sentences based on their own experiences.

When I realized that my gifted students would be seeing vocabulary testing as a part of the PSAT and SAT, I tried to introduce more vocabulary words, not only in the form of lessons, but as a part of my own vocabulary. With the instructions, "If I use a word that you do not know, it is your responsibility to ask me or to find out on your own what I mean," I tried to help them master words seldom used by themselves or their peers. I think this procedure helped some.

Toward the end of my teaching career, a district administrator, Dr. Cathy Rideout, gave all teachers in the district a word a week, asking them to integrate it into their own vocabularies so that students could learn from their contextual use. If a teacher used a word over and over in his/her delivery, I am sure some students learned its meaning; however, I always wondered how many teachers followed up with this request. I tried to do this consistantly.

TEACHING GRAMMAR

I do not believe I ever taught a grammar lesson that many of my students did not have this comment: "No one has ever taught me this." Of course, I knew that every teacher teaches grammar, starting with the eight parts of speech. The problem is that every lesson on each part of speech was not stored in a properly labeled permanent file folder. If it had been, then the cumulative learning would have had students coming to me knowing exactly what an introductory adverbial, subordinate clause is. Instead, their response when I mentioned one was always "A what?"

Many funny things happened as a result of my grammar lessons. I witnessed many epiphanies as students declared, "Oh, now I see what you are talking about." One particular Horn student, Blake Adams, a perfectionist who wanted always to be on top of learning, was so frustrated because he just could not get sentence analysis down pat, that I truly thought he was going to have a coronary, yet he finally got to the point of total understanding. Many grammatical errors have become common, including some made by very well educated people, but when my students discovered that something was wrong grammatically, it became hard for them to sit still and not to call attention to the error. For instance, Blake, this same student who was so perplexed at first, later came to class telling me, "My dad told me that if I corrected him one more time, he was going to backhand me!"

Every English teacher has his list of grammar errors he/she finds it hard to tolerate. One of mine involves pronoun antecedent agreement. And, of course, this disagreement is probably the most common error made, even by the "so-called" well educated. The pronouns "everybody" and "everyone" give the most trouble. When one of these words is used in a sentence, the pronouns that follow must be singular in order to agree with either of them because they, too, are singular. "Everybody" means every one body, and "everyone" means every single one; therefore, a sentence should read "Everyone needs to remember to bring <u>his</u> book to class," and not "Everyone needs to remember to bring <u>their</u> book to class." The use of "farther" vs. "further" and other such mix-ups are on many teachers' lists. But I have to tell you this. I worked at a bank for about nine years early in my adult life. I worked in the loan department as a secretary to an officer who lent money to people with needs or wants; however, I had to become an English teacher before I learned that one "lends," not "loans," money. The money he lends is called a "loan." In other words, the verb is "lend," and the noun is "loan." Another example, which I often shared with my students, is from a time that I reviewed teachers for a test the State of Texas decided all teachers needed to take to prove their efficiency as teachers. Many who taught subjects other than English and math, which are what this test included, were concerned that they might have trouble since they had not been schooled on these subjects for such a long time. This was the reason why I was doing the English review. One night after a lesson on "good vs. well," a North Mesquite coach, Gary Childress, came up to me and said, "Thank you for this lesson. For years I have told my players that they played good. Now I realize they weren't playing good at all; they were playing well."

I do not think grammar lessons should ever stop. There are so many words that we confuse and therefore misuse, and if we want to be considered "learned," we should continue working to eliminate such errors. Book stores are full of books that can help with this. They usually have the term "confusing words" or a similar term as part of their titles. I still learn from such books, and I always feel better about myself once I have resolved such confusion.

The Vanishing Art of Letter Writing

In this highly technical world, many of my old favorites have gone by the wayside. Letter writing is one of these. We call, we text, we email, but seldom do we sit down and write personal letters. Some of my great treasures are letters that I have received over my lifetime, so I thought the thing for me to do as a school teacher was to require my students to write letters with the idea that perhaps I could stir up some renewed interest.

I modeled letter writing for them, sending them at least two or three letters over each summer, some just to say hello, some for a stronger purpose. Many students proclaimed how much they looked forward to my letters, some saying that they were the first personal mail that they had ever received.

One year during something the postal service dreamed up called "National Letter Writing Day," I assigned my students the job of writing a personal letter to someone they knew. I explained that it could be to a friend who had moved away, a cousin, or even to a grandparent. I went on to say that grandparents love getting attention from their grandchildren, and since most grandparents' days are numbered, perhaps that would be a really good choice for some of them. One student, Brian Cain, after about ten minutes spent composing his letter, brought it to me for approval. It said, "Dear Grandma. My English teacher said that I should write you a letter before you die. . ." Needless to say, I laughed until I cried. His grandmother, however, told me that she cherished that very special letter from her grandson, in spite of (if not because of) its humor.

LEADERSHIP TRAINING

L eadership training was a perfect fit for my humanities-based language arts curriculum. Gifted students are all leaders in some ways. Some are leaders because of their scholarly ability. They serve as models for other students; therefore, they are leaders even if they are not verbally gifted. Most of my students coming into the gifted program, however, were excellent leadership candidates because they exhibited almost all of the characteristics of leaders.

I did see a need to add information on leadership early in the history of this gifted curriculum. I had students keep a notebook so that they could keep up with all the good materials provided. I had Dr. John Horn, now retired from being superintendent of our district, as a guest speaker on a couple of occasions because of his leadership acumen.

Very popular with my students were trips to Camp Grady Spruce at Possum Kingdom Lake and later to a camp in Collin County for a weekend of leadership training by YMCA personnel. Many activities convinced my students that they were, indeed, all leaders. Then they were given instructions and practice on how to maximize their effectiveness as leaders in many situations. I was very impressed with the quality of the instruction at both camps but in particularly, the Collin County camp.

One year, another leadership activity involved listening to a panel of community leaders tell of how they use their leadership skills in the workplace. I served as moderator to a very effective group including some of my ex-students who have become successful in the professional world: Christian Rodriguez and Jonathan Neerman; some parents of current and former students: Tony Apel, Karl Kutch, Judy Pardun, James Gaskin, Mike Kovar, and Mark Hindman; and other local professionals: Jenice Johnson, Jan Julian, Mary Randall, and Mark Reid. This was a big hit because students could hear success stories, literally, from "the horses' mouths."

From our study of Machiavelli's *The Prince*, we got to see a style of leadership that, although it may be effective, is not the style of which we approve. Students decided that such premises as "the end justifies the means" and other such Machiavellian concepts were void of moral turpitude, therefore, not ideal for a moral world. This study did allow all of us to recognize and to understand better the political implications of such concepts as seen in society today.

Some of the best instruction came on the way to the Collin County camp one year. Our then mayor, Mike Anderson, and one of the city's administrators, Carol Zolnerowich, met us at the school district's Professional Development Center (PDC) for a session on how our city operates. After distributing an organizational chart, Ms. Z (as she is called) explained how everything works together for the benefit of the citizens. She also gave us a list of ways citizens, even teenagers, can serve the city. She also explained, as did the Mayor, how important it is for citizens to be involved in community service. Many class projects aiding Mesquite Social Services were born of this seminar.

Another way my students learned about leadership was through my "Write to Publish" project. This was an every-six-weeks assignment for a long time in my classes. After focusing on how important it is to be well versed on a given subject before speaking out, I tried to convince students to share their ideas with others.

One way to do this is to write letters to the editor of a newspaper, hoping to get them published. Many of my students published, some more than once. I mounted the letter and a picture of each student fortunate enough to have his/her letter chosen. These colorful placards became a permanent decoration for my classroom walls each year for at least twenty of my twenty-eight years. Once I tried to stop the project, but students had a fit. They sort of liked the attention given them, not to mention the colorful wall that everyone noticed. Several students have published letters and essays after their days in my class. I have even had parents publish once they saw their children could. I always tried to publish, myself, in order to model what I wanted them to do. Some times one of my letters was accepted; sometimes, not. But my students always knew that I was trying, as they were.

Leadership training was an excellent way for my students to see that with giftedness come responsibilities. I wanted to send my students out into the world prepared to make it a better place, not just for themselves, but also for others. More importantly, I wanted them to see that because they are so capable, they have a responsibility to use their leadership skills in this way.

ADDING SOCIAL STUDIES. . .

The inclusion of social studies into my gifted curriculum was one of the easiest of all the humanities to integrate. Government, in particular, was a natural choice to add. After all, there is just so much that can be taught in a one-semester government class. This left me lots of areas to choose for a focus, so when I finally made the decision to include government, I chose what I considered the most important: local government.

The most successful way I did this was to focus on local government as an introduction to my Leadership Unit. As I mentioned before, I invited the mayor and one of the city department heads to come and talk to my students about several things: how the city operates, how the council operates, how the many departments of the city operate, among other things. They gave us handouts including the organizational chart of the city operation, a list of ways citizens can serve, and volunteer opportunities that exist for all citizens, including teenagers. Even I learned much from this presentation. I only wish I had included it much earlier.

This knowledge of one's city's operation is something that I think every adult should pursue. The information is there for the asking.

History was even easier, particularly since we read the classics. A little historical background made each classic so much more enjoyable, and with history being my minor, it was fun to research and share such history. Also, particularly during the American strand, our complete study followed a chronological path, for to separate the history of America from American literature would have been impossible. So many of the early American pieces of literature were based on need and circumstance. The early ship logs of immigrants coming to our shores, the letters they wrote to friends and family in the Old World, the planting charts they established (which later were incorporated into what we now call almanacs), the government documents, and the list goes on, are all history interwoven with the literature of the times. I did assign many of my classes an historical family research project where they were to find out what traits they have and from which side of the family they were inherited. They also traced their family tree for several generations as part of this assignment. Sometime, but not always, I also had them research the source of their own names.

I always wanted to incorporate some geography into my curriculum because I am appalled at how little our young people know about geography. When they added world geography to the list of required subjects, I was ecstatic;

however, seldom does a world geography teacher have time to narrow the scope of coverage to the area in which we live. I dreamed of getting maps of Texas, Dallas, and Mesquite (and these all do exist and are available free) to share with my students and to build lessons around. At the time I had these students, each was getting a driver's license and what an ideal time to acquaint them with their immediate surroundings. I never got to the point where I had time to do this; however, this past Christmas, I went to the Texas Highway Department and got copies of the latest Texas and Dallas maps for my grown children's stockings, something they all appreciated.

Having spent nine years as a bank employee, I realized early the need to understand how a checking account works, how to balance a bank statement each month, what the best way is to save money, how to apply for a loan (such as for college costs), how to avoid abusing credit, and what kind of investment opportunities a bank has available. There are so many adults who still have no idea how beneficial this kind of information could be, yet it would be valuable information for them. These are specialized topics that aren't covered in any high school course, economics included, and I would have loved to include these little economic lessons in my curriculum. But time never allowed it.

History Lessons from Fiction

Having majored in English and minored in history, I love the genre called "historical fiction." A good story placed in the middle of or around some historical event or era always gives the reader a better understanding of that time period. This is probably the reason why I chose many of the classics for my student reading list.

Lots of things can be learned about the wars America has been a part of from reading fiction set in war times. One can understand the **French American War** much better after having read Cooper's *Last of the Mohicans*. America of the **Civil War** era is beautifully represented in a number of the books I taught. We see a little of life during that time from a different perspective, those left behind to tend to the home front, in Faulkner's *The Unvanquished*. We learn the horrors of war, particular one where soldiers were often teenagers, from reading Crane's *Red Badge of Courage*. Love and life on the battlefield during **World War I** are seen and

Remarque's   _oops!_

better understood from reading Hemingway's _A Farewell to Arms_, and reading ~~DeMarque's~~ _All Quiet on the Western Front_ shows us that life on the battlefield is no different for the enemy. From the short story collection _The Things They Carried_ by O'Brien, we get an unusual look at the **Vietnam War**.

Other American history lessons abound in the books we read, some related to the ills of our society. Hawthorne's _The Scarlet Letter_ and Arthur Miller's _The Crucible_ show us the hypocrisy that was so much a part of early America. We see the horrors of discrimination in Lee's _To Kill a Mockingbird_, Gaines' _A Lesson Before Dying_, and Ellison's _The Invisible Man_. The unique problems associated with the Great Depression of the 1930s and the Dust Bowl era are a part of Steinbeck's _The Grapes of Wrath_ and _Of Mice and Men_. A look at misplaced values in the changing scene of twentieth-century American life can be seen in Fitzgerald's _The Great Gatsby_ and Miller's _Death of a Salesman_.

We get a great look at the Renaissance period in Europe by reading Stone's _The Agony and the Ecstasy_. It is an excellent depiction of the role the church played in that society. It also gives us much information about early art history. Shakespeare's works, though embellished by his creative mind, enhance our knowledge of the era of Julius Caesar, his rise and fall, as well as the ever-changing rule of England based on religion from many of his other plays. We learned about Apartied from reading selections from Mathabane's _Kaffir Boy_, and we better understood colonization of Africa by the missionaries through our study of *Things Fall Apart* by Achebe.

These lessons in history that come from reading the classics is just one more reason for reading them. And while including a good story may disallow a book's validity as "history," it does make the valid facts that are included much more memorable.

WHY FOCUS ON ART?

There are many reasons why one's education should include learning about art. To understand why I supported the inclusion of art in my curriculum, I am sharing my lesson on art appreciation.

Here are some of the reasons why learning about art is important:

1. Art has been a part of our lives from our earliest beginnings. How do we know this? Remember the cave drawings?

2. The ability to express ourselves in art sets us apart from all other living things. Surely you don't believe strapping a paint brush to an elephant's tusk and letting him splash paint on a canvas really says that the elephant knows he is painting a masterpiece. Recently I read that his owner was claiming this.

3. Art is an integral part of our lives. We see it in our museums, our doctors' offices, and we put it on the

walls of our home. Newspapers have a section that covers art, and our schools teach it. It is definitely a big part of our lives.

4. To be of interest to other people is still another reason. I really like this one. Walter Pater once said, "To know when one's self is interested, is the first condition of interesting other people." I believe that this is true. Knowing about famous works of art gives us not only an edge, it gives us a way to interest others in what we know. Art is the same everywhere, so like music, it is almost a universal language. It is a great conversation piece because it evokes feelings and opinions, and they don't have to be the same as other people's.

What Exactly Is a Work of Art?

Art is an expression of an idea. It is visual language. Skilled artists utilize the elements and the principles of art to express themselves. These elements and principles are the alphabet of visual language. Artistic expression occurs when the urge to communicate is linked with originality, the knowledge of structure, and the ability to manipulate the medium chosen. Art enables one to express his or her own creativity through a nonverbal form of communication.

Does this mean that to benefit from art, we have to be artists ourselves? Absolutely not. Knowing what art is and how it works can benefit all of us greatly.

- As we become aware of the artistic accomplishments of other cultures, we learn and understand those cultures better. We can even make connections with those cultures in order to better understand ourselves. By making connections, we can sometimes claim a part of that culture as our own.

- Art improves the quality of our lives by giving us an enriched environment. By selecting certain paintings and pictures for our own homes, we make our environment more enjoyable. Buildings or homes are improved by the interesting and beautiful works of art all can enjoy. Most often, this is enrichment beyond the purpose of our visit.

- By studying the similarities and differences of old and new art, we can better understand our own lives because art history is our history.

- Art gives us a continuing learning opportunity and challenge. There is no end to what we can learn. . .

    about life
    about ourselves
    about our history
    about other cultures
    about how we connect to other cultures
    about art in general
    about a specific work of art

. . .simply by giving art a chance to make an impact on our lives.

The knowledge of art among young people today is most often slim, if not nil. Even those who take art in school are often so focused on the skill of producing it that they don't realize the importance of it in their lives.

I have given many reasons why art should be a focus of educaton. If you have never even thought of art and its relationship to you, hopefully you will begin to see it in a different way.

This is What It Takes:

1. You must give yourself time to see what is there.
2. You must interact in many ways, looking for. . .

    a. possible movement suggested
    b. shapes and lines that stand out
    c. contrasts/comparisons that are obvious
    d. color/color scheme (different, unusual, particularly pleasing)
    e. details
    f. content/story of the painting (Use your imagination to fill in
    g. the blanks if none is obvious.)
    h. symbols
    i. time frame
    j. place
    k. history lessons
    l. connections to your own experience

m. connection to and appropriateness of title (Guessing before you look sometimes helps with this.)

n. personal opinion/personal taste

You must practice this skill of interacting with art. The best way is to go to an art museum, giving yourself plenty of time to interact with several paintings. Once you do this, I believe the answers to these questions will reflect that you have an educated opinion of art.

The Questions to Answer:

Do you see the benefits of having knowledge of art?
Do you see how art can broaden your base of knowledge?
Do you know what knowledge of art says about your level of culture?
Do you understand that knowledge of art can even make you a more interesting person?

If the answer is "yes" to any of these questions, then I will consider you on the path to an enriched life.

Much of what I have shared here was gathered as I taught the humanities-based Renaissance English classes at North Mesquite High School and more recently, John Horn High School during the last eighteen or so years of my twenty-nine-year teaching career. I, like my students in years past, learned much from a good friend and former parent, Kathy Lawrence, who always volunteered to come from her teaching art job in the Richardson ISD to conduct art seminars every three years at both North and Horn high schools.

But most of what I say comes from my heart. It comes from my own personal experience with art (for it has touched me personally) and with my observation of how much the study of art has touched my students of the past. We grew together in this thing called "art appreciation," experiencing every benefit of which I have spoken. I had many objectives during my tenure as a teacher, but getting students to see the benefits of making art a part of their lives was an important one. I believe I speak for most of them and myself when I say that interacting with art has and will continue to enhance our lives.

LIFE LESSONS FROM LITERATURE

One of the major focuses of any piece of literature ever studied in or for my class was what could be learned about life from being exposed to its content. Although this is not all that was ever discussed about any of the books we read, here is an example of such a focus for several of the classics.

Hawthorne's *The Scarlet Letter* was a challenge for every group of my students to read, yet there are some worthwhile lessons in its pages. Hawthorne was a master of character development. His main characters are all very well developed, meaning that the readers' opinions of each, changes from the beginning of the book to the end. Ironically, in this book, opinions change 180 degrees. We start out frowning at Hester for her behavior and feeling sorry for her husband. We admire the Reverend for his leadership and concern for Pearl. We shake our heads at Pearl's impudent behavior. But by the end of the story, we forgive and admire Hester, we despise her husband for his wickedness, we dislike the reverend for his lack of backbone, and we finally see and can appreciate Pearl, a mature young lady who loves her mother. What do we learn from just this? Perhaps we should be slow to judge. We can never know the circumstances; therefore, perhaps we shouldn't judge at all. Of course, there are other embedded lessons we can also relate to life today, but this was always my focus.

Steinbeck's *Of Mice and Men* illustrates just as many (if not more) of life's lessons. Through the characters of Crooks and Curley's wife, we understand the horrible effects of loneliness and isolation by seeing both sides of discrimination. In Carlson, we see the insensitivity some people have toward others, which, in turn, reminds us to be sensitive to others' feelings. In Slim, we observe a great role model, a person who understands how to be a leader whom all can respect. George models the perfect friend for us. He remains responsible for his friend Lennie, who cannot be responsible for himself.

Gilgamesh, the oldest written work known to man, is also a great story about friendship, but the greatest benefit for readers is its revelation of the grief process. By observing the main character as he goes through the various stages of grief, the reader becomes aware that all of these stages are normal and even necessary for recovery. This story also reminds us that life on Earth is indeed finite.

Plato's *Symposium* is a hard read, but it is a philosophical way of approaching an understanding of established virtues and moral values. It supports Lew Wallace's "Beauty is in the eye of the beholder" by showing us that "Love is in the heart of the lover." Through Socrates' and his friends' discussion of the definition of love, we see that it is many things, or rather, that there are many kinds of love and that each person views it in a different way.

From Homer's *Odyssey*, we are exposed to the benefits of patience through the character of Penelope, paternal love and loyalty through Telemacus, and bravery, tenacity, and persistence through Odysseus. Of course, we also learn from Odysseus' shortcomings. When he brags to Poseidon, we see the bad effects of excessive ego. We even see the negative effects of drug-induced stupors when the sailors are influenced by the Lotus Eaters.

Through the main character of Fitzgerald's *The Great Gatsby*, one sees the ills of trying to be someone he is not. We learn that wealth does not make a person happy nor does it necessarily make one acceptable. Through many of Fitzgerald's characters, we see the shallowness of the "new rich," so characteristic of this time in American history, the 1920s.

Mark Twain's *The Adventures of Huckleberry Finn* is the story of a young boy's life during early America, but it is also a lesson in discrimination. We see the relationship between Huck and Jim grow into a meaningful friendship in a time when it was not acceptable for "black" and "white" to associate. By having all the bad guys white men and Jim, the black man of the story, portrayed as Huck's hero, Twain reminds us that we should not judge another person by the color of his skin.

Of course, this is just a "tiny tip of the iceberg." By the end of their junior year, my students had been assigned approximately forty classics to read and to be able to discuss. There are so many great classics that I taught over the years, and there is so much to learn about life from reading them. Of course, there are many more good reasons for reading quality literature, but the applying of its content to our own lives is a meaningful and worthwhile experience.

WITH FRIENDSHIP COMES RESPONSIBILITY

One of the most, if not <u>the</u> most, enjoyed novel I assigned my students is John Steinbeck's *Of Mice and Men*. Before they ever opened the book, they were, of course, impressed with its size. Once they opened it, they also liked that it is so easy to read and to understand. That is, until they really started thinking about it. Then it became much more complex. There are just so many life lessons that can be learned from this book!

One such lesson is that to be isolated is "hell"! There is just no better way to say it. Curley's wife, who happens to be the only female on the ranch, has been given orders not to talk to the men. This leaves only her new husband (whom she really doesn't like very much, much less love) for her to communicate with. She slips around and manages to talk to Slim, who has more confidence than fear, and to Lenny, which ultimately costs her greatly. She tells us in no uncertain terms that being lonely is the worst fate one can have.

Crooks, the stable guy, has the same "hell" of a life. He is isolated from many of the areas the other hands frequent. No one wants to appear too friendly to a black man, and he is often "put in his place" for being the wrong color. This life of isolation is his own private hell. From this scenario we learn that we should never be guilty of isolating another human being, that we should be accepting of others, even those who are different than we are.

Probably the most important lesson that one can learn from reading this book is that friendship requires responsibility. It requires sacrifice; it requires compromise; it requires tough love at times. It always requires unconditional acceptance. We see this in the life that George has chosen with Lennie. It also means "covering each other's back," which we see not only in George's looking out for Lennie (who cannot really look out for himself) but also in Lennie's anger when he thinks someone is talking bad about his friend, George. From this book, students analyze their own friendships, determining which of their friends could be considered only "fair-weather friends" and who are "the real McCoys."

Some pretty big lessons were learned from such a small book!

JUST TRIPPING ALONG

As soon as I realized it was an option that I could make happen, I took my students on field trips. Sometimes the trip was to see a live play, and over the course of twenty-eight years, we saw some really good ones. *Of Mice and Men* and *To Kill a Mockingbird* were outstanding, as was almost every Shakespeare play we saw. We went to the Dallas Theater Center (both locations) many times, to Southern Methodist University, to the University of Dallas, to the Collin County Community College, to Theatre Three, and to the McKinney Avenue Contemporary Theater (the MAC). Wherever a play was playing that I thought age-appropriate, that is where we went. Of course, sometimes my "thinking" it was age appropriate proved to be wrong. I will never forget seeing a really risque version of Hamlet at SMU. If the buses had not left to park quite a distance away, we would have left the theater after the first scene. I have never seen such a suggestive play before or since. My fellow teacher, Lynne Hager, was really embarrassed because she, as the then senior AP teacher, invited my freshmen, sophomore, and junior students and me to join the trip, not knowing what was in store. I remember talking all the way home about what had happened and why it was unacceptable. I think the kids were more interested in our embarrassment than they were in the risque play we had taken them to see.

For many years, I designed a family outing. One year it was to see *Dinah Was,* a play about the life of the singer Dinah Washington. It, too, had quite a raunchy scene in it, but it was such an outstanding play, nobody complained (although there was a lot of squirming going on during that particular scene).

But I didn't stop at just plays. Over the years we also attended operas, ballet performances, symphony concerts, and even a one-woman show. Some of these were on our own; some were through the TITAS organization. For many years, I took my students to the Student Forums related to the Tate Lecture Series at SMU. The students and chaperons got to see many well-know news anchors (such as George Stephanopolis and Walter Cronkite), famous authors (such as Tom Clancy and John Grisham), movie stars (Julie Andrews, for one), VIP's of government (such as Nelson Mandela, Al Gore, and Bob Dole), great scientists, business leaders and many other noteworthy individuals.

We sometimes just went to the MISD Professional Development Center (the PDC) in order to spend a whole day working on a specific task. Some of these workshops were related to students appreciating fine art, learning about our city government, and finding out how to publish their writing, to name a few. Some years I also took my students to the Dallas Arboretum for a photography symposium. In fact, one year our trip there was delayed a couple of weeks because right before we were to leave, 9–11 happened, and our plans were quickly cancelled. I was so thankful that I had all my students with me in the multi-purpose room where we sat glued to the television that morning. I think they felt safer there among their friends and with me and the chaperons, and I was glad we could discuss the catastrophe before the students were released to go back to their classrooms.

I took my Advanced Texas Studies class to Austin one year. That was a real challenge because the class was a semester only, and I had only had them a month before the trip. I learned then that to take an overnight trip, I needed to know my students really well, and I had to have their respect. It was a good trip, however, because the then representative from Mesquite, Rep. Bill Blackwell, met with us and showed us around the capitol.

Once I started teaching the gifted and talented program and having the students for three years, I felt very comfortable offering spring break trips. I started with a trip to New York City, and it was one to remember. While there, the "worst blizzard of the century" occurred, and we were so lucky to get there before it started and to have left after it thawed. We were also lucky that only one change to the itinerary had to be made: we had to substitute the Natural History Museum for the Museum of Fine Arts. Because we had planned to travel mostly by subway, the snow was not a problem. In fact, the students had a blast with the one foot of snow that we never see in Texas. Our bus trip to Upper Manhattan was almost a disaster, but we had a great driver. Our breathing fogged up the windows, which made it hard to see the sites he described, but we made it to all our intended stops. I will never forget arriving at St. John the Divine Episcopal Church. The driver warned us to watch for things flying through the air (such as trash can lids) because the wind was so strong. When my daughter and I stepped out of the church to return to the bus, we stepped out into twelve inches of snow with shoes that were not appropriate for such weather. We had an umbrella that we were holding over us, but the wind caught it and turned it upside down, something I had seen in comic strips but never experienced. I got so tickled at that point because I thought to myself, "Here I am with over sixty kids, thousands of miles from home, in the worst blizzard of the century, worrying about flying trashcan lids. I must be crazy!" It turned out so great, however, that this was the first of many trips to NYC. Another highlight was that one of my student's luggage got lost. This was the first and only time this happened in all the years of taking these trips. Mike Moran was only a freshman then and pretty embarrassed by the fact that he didn't even have one change of clothes. His friends quickly volunteered to share their shirts, and the chaperons bought him several pairs of underwear and socks so that his trip wasn't a complete fiasco. From then on, I always insisted that at least one change of clothes be packed in the carry-on bag. The highlights of the NY trip were for students to see at least two Broadway shows, visit the Statue of Liberty and Ellis Island, go atop the Empire State Building, tour the Radio City Music Hall, spend time at the Metropolitan Art Museum, walk through the Wall Street district, and later, go to the 9-11 scene. In fact, one of the trips to NYC landed us there exactly six months after the 9-11 attack, and we were atop the Empire State Building when the beams of light from the site were turned on. One of the worst scenes I have ever experienced was walking around the attack area and seeing scraps of clothing on the branches of surrounding trees.

The next year, since the focus for the whole year was American literature and humanities, I decided to take them to Washington, D.C. This trip was also a fabulous experience for my students, and we continued to make it to D.C. during every American-strand year until I retired. There were many highlights to this trip, also, including the Holocaust Museum, all the Smithsonian museums, the Capitol, the White House, the monuments, and all the other historical buildings. A trip to a suburban dinner theater was always a highlight, too, since we no longer have dinner theater productions available here in Dallas. Another highlight was the famous long-running play "Shear Madness."

The third long trip I took my students on was to Granbury, Texas. We only stayed one night, but we saw "Dracula" at the Granbury Opry House, went to the animal preserve at Fossil Rim, saw the Dinosaur tracks in the area, and toured the Granbury primitive jail and other buildings from an era long past. This proved to be no match for the other trips, but they seem to enjoy the two-day weekend at the time..

The next time I taught the three curriculum strands, Granbury left the rotation because I got permission to add Florida's Disney World. It was a pretty hard "sell," but I finally convinced Dr. Horn, the then superintendent of schools, that we were going for the Y.E.S. (Youth Education Seminar) program, not just for the amusement part of the park venue. During the Disney World trips, we got to go early, not only to beat the crowds but also to see behind and under the scenes of many of the rides and displays, to attend lessons on animation, perform improvisation theater, conduct scientific experiments, explore related careers, and the list goes on. We visited every park and then went to the campground area where we saw a great show, Hoop-de-do, that also included the best food of the trip. I will never forget the audience participation there by one of our chaperons, Glenn Bennett, who made a darling ballerina in his pink tutu.

The last trip to New York was quite different. When it was time to return to Mesquite, there was turbulent weather between NYC and DFW. This cancellation of flights for our group of approximately 160 students, parents, and chaperons, could have been a disaster; however, World Strides, our student travel company, came to our rescue. After the seniors made their flight, World Strides transported the rest of us to a brand new hotel on Staten Island that had big rooms with fantastic beds. We were fed well and entertained until we finally got everyone home. By leaving a few at a time, as room on flights could be found, some of the students had to spend extra days/nights before getting home. Of course, one group got to go by Staten Island ferry back to Chinatown shopping, so they weren't too upset about the delay. In fact, many of the seniors (the first group to leave) were disappointed because they didn't get to stay the extra two or three days. Needless to say, I didn't rest until everyone was home, safe and sound.

I hate that these trips are no longer offered. The school district felt that my retirement was a good time to retire the trips, also. I know that much of what my students will remember about my class is related to the many field trips we took. They were all fast-paced and filled from early morning to late night, but everyone always seem to accept that he got his money's worth. Just seeing the students taking in all the sites that they had previously only seen on the television screen was worth all my effort, and in spite of several bouts of virus, sore throats, and runny noses that seemed to crop up during almost every trip, I managed to survive all the nursing duties and to have fun myself.

MONEY, MONEY EVERYWHERE

I had a teacher in high school who once told me that I should be a lawyer. Her rationale was that I was good at motivating others to do things. But two other teachers of mine told me that I should major in finance. There was a reason for this.

During the 1950s at Mesquite High School, the Football Sweetheart was not chosen by the football team, nor was the FFA Sweetheart chosen by members of the Future Farmers of America. Instead, both organizations ordered a contest between the four grade levels. A penny represented a vote, and whichever class could raise the most money got its candidate elected as sweetheart.

The president of our class, Walter Wheat, was pretty smart when he appointed me as the Promotion Chairman of our class for all four years of our high school experience. If there is one thing I can do (other than to teach), it is to raise money. Our candidates won seven of the eight contests during those four years.

My philosophy about money is that it is only good for supplying what you need or want. I never have been a hoarder of money. When I started to junior high school, my mother and daddy started giving me an allowance. With the money they gave me, I learned to find a way to buy and to do just about everything I desired. Sometimes I would lend fifty cents or a dollar to a friend and charge a quarter interest. This was a real bonus for me, allowing me to buy gifts and to go places that my budget did not include. As I got older, and my allowance increased, I would lend more money and earn more interest. Even before this, when I was in about the fifth or sixth grade, I can remember picking up soft drink bottles along the highway where we lived and cashing them in for two cents each in order to be able to go to the Saturday matinee movie in downtown Mesquite. When I asked if I could go somewhere or do something or buy something, it was common for Mother to say, "You can if you can afford it." Throughout my early adult life, when I wanted something I could not afford, I would just decide what I could live without, organize a garage sale, and "voila," I soon had the money I needed. Obviously, I credit my mother for endowing me with the ability to raise money.

This is one of the things I always tried to get over to my students. I demonstrated for them how this works every time there is a need for money, whether for a community service project or for a trip to New York City, Washington D.C., or Disney World. I always told them, "Don't let money stand in the way of your doing what you need or want to do.

Just get busy and make it happen." I also encouraged them not to ask their parents for this extra money. I truly believe that a person, more often than not, appreciates things more (and consequently, enjoys the experience more) when he, himself, has paid for it.

When I first organized trips out of the state for my gifted and talented students, I knew that the quality of the trip I wanted to sponsor would be costly. Dr. James Terry, the superintendent at the time, told me that I had permission to take these trips, only if I could offer a way that all students could go. This meant that I had to have lots of fund-raising activities so that a student whose parents could not afford to contribute could raise all the money himself. This was a challenge that I accepted because I knew that I had been successful at raising lots of money in the past.

Among the fundraisers I selected for my students were the usual: selling candy, cookies, nuts, Christmas items, candles, promotional calendars, safety kits, and magazine subscriptions, and those who were determined always did well selling these items. Where my students made the most, though, was at the multi-family garage sales we had each year on the weekend before or after Labor Day weekend. Each participant was assigned a number that he used to mark his items to sell. In addition to getting one hundred percent of this income, based on a point system he could get a portion of what we made selling drinks and cookies and raffling off baked goods. It was not unusual for a student to make as much as fifty percent of the cost of a trip just at the garage sale. It was a great time and place to establish the camaraderie that I so wanted my students to experience. I will never forget the cheesecakes I snatched from the arms of parent Lisa Newton before she took them to the bakery raffle. My mouth waters just thinking about them. Parents were a big part of the success of this event because we relied on them to bake the cookies and raffle baked good, furnish the drinks, and even work at the event. But it was such a fun time, and all of us who put our "junk" into the sale had fun selecting and bringing others' junk home with us. Part of these "finds" are exactly what went into next year's sale, just under a different number.

After the garage sale, the second most successful fundraiser was the silent auction/talent show which we usually had in November. To participate in this fund-raiser, one had to furnish at least two items for the auction, a batch of cookies, and pay $1.00 participation fee which paid for the punch we served. There were a few other requirements for full refund, but those who met them all received one hundred percent of the money for tickets they sold to the event. We usually threw in a raffle for something like tickets to a professional sporting event, and they also got the money for tickets they sold as part of their "earnings."

I loved this, mainly because it was a chance to see some talent that no one knew about. When senior Martin Uwah sang and accompanied himself on the piano, no one had any idea that he had such talent. And this is just one example. Over the years, we saw fantastic instrumentals (violin, piano, guitar, drums, bands, and concert groups), fantastic choral offerings (solos, duets, trios, etc), dance numbers (solos, including break dancing, and groups), comic routines (solos and groups), skits, interpretive readings, martial arts demonstrations, and more. Among the most entertaining were the many parodies (songs, poems, skits) that poked fun at me, such as the Leos family's "The Muhl Days of Christmas" and a random group of singers' "A Muhlet Carol." But the one that floored me was the group of Sara/Sarah's who made fun of my inability to keep them straight. I just wish it had been shot with a video camera so that I could continue laughing hysterically at those girls, led by Sara (or is it Sarah?) Allen, whose song and dance entertained us all.

I continue to raise money and/or collect items so that I can participate in community service activities in and around Mesquite. The group called the "Who" has done this several times in the past year, and it gives all of us a great feeling as well as helping those in need. I still have garage sales occasionally, but now it is more to help others with a need or a wish than to realize capital for my own benefit.

Also, I am a newly elected member to the Mesquite Education Foundation Board, and guess what my major responsibility is? It is to gather items for a silent auction that is part of our big fund-raising Gala held each spring. I guess I will never be able to quit asking others for donations. My husband says, "Just quit being good at it." Okay, all right, already!

SPECIAL ACTIVITIES, PROJECTS, AND PRODUCTS

M any people have a hard time believing all that my humanities-based English class included. There are probably others, but the following activities and projects and their resulting products readily come to my mind:

1. Readers Theater presentations in conjunction with the study of mythology
2. Group symposiums following the study of Plato's *Symposium*
3. American author notebooks
4. Poetry notebooks
5. Leadership notebooks
6. Leadership guest panel
7. War veterans guest panel
8. Leadership Weekend trips
9. Granbury Weekend trip
10. Spring break trips to New York City

11. Spring break trips to Washington, D.C.
12. Editorial Workshops at the PDC
13. Art Appreciation Workshops
14. Photography project (at the PDC or the Arboretum)
15. Field trips to theater productions
16. Trips to the opera
17. Trips to various TITUS performances
18. Warm fuzzy exchange at Christmas
19. Music Appreciation guest lecturer
20. All-night lock-in at end of year
21. Saturday Supper Club meetings
22. Design-your-own food collection project
23. Dollar tree project that ended up raising over $3,000. charity project
24. Search for Meaning notebooks
25. Family genealogy chart
26. Family gene tracing activity
27. Map of life after study of Homer's *Odyssey*
28. Various activities following the reading of Steinbeck's *Of Mice and Men*
29. Focus on American art and artists (each student had a different artist to master)
30. Focus on World art and artists (each student had a different artist to master)
31. Mini-reports (subjects varied by year)
32. Vertical teams (for a variety of purposes)
33. Reading buddies
34. Presentation of famous quotations

35. Paraphrasing and/or parodying adages
36. Writing sonnets
37. Composing other poetry
38. Designing t-shirts (representing self)
39. Designing totem poles (representing one's life)
40. Parodying songs/poems
41. Humanities appreciation notebooks
42. Trip notebooks
43. Tub corrections
44. Write to Publish assignments
45. Diagramming sentences
46. Learning poetry scansion
47. End of the year parties
48. Garage sale for raising trip money
49. Silent auction and talent shows for raising trip money
50. Other fund raisers: selling candy, cookies, magazines, nuts, Christmas stuff, calendars, etc
51. Spring meeting for new students' parents
52. Ordering books for next year
53. Writing advice to new students
54. Participating in the PTA contests each year
55. Entering annual contest sponsored by Eastfield College (money prizes)
56. Entering various other contests (poetry and essays)
57. Keeping up the composition folders
58. Annual Christmas party
59. Vocabulary word presentation

60. Keeping up the "Noteworthy Literature I Have Experienced" list
61. Keeping personal resume updated
62. Timed writings
63. Research project
64. Writing of personal essays
65. Manners lessons
66. *The Velveteen Rabbit* project
67. Board of Director's Table exercise
68. The project that emulated *The Dallas Morning News* focus on an individual each Sunday, called "High Profile"
69. Pen-pal project with school in Pennsylvania
70. Pen-pal project focused on fear with elementary school students at Shands Elementary School (taught by my cousin, Debbie Johnson)
71. Design of children's activity page for Easter published in the *Mesquite News*
72. Participation in Student Voices and Teacher Voices of *The Dallas Morning News*

V

SIDE DISHES

Sponsoring Cheerleading

At the end of my second year of teaching, my principal, Mr. Bud Campbell, asked me to take over sponsorship of the cheerleading squad. I had mixed emotions about this because as a teacher, I often resented their being taken out of my class for such things as showing people around the school. I disliked some of the disparaging things I had heard about some of the girls, and I felt as if they needed more discipline. However, always up for a challenge, I decided that I would take on this responsibility providing Mr. Campbell would let me work on some rules for behavior and a better way of conducting try-outs. He agreed, so I took over all three squads shortly after they had been chosen and right before the end of school when they would be going to camp.

At first, I felt I had been dumped into the middle of a hornet's nest. The girls who had already been cheerleaders missed the old sponsor, and they greatly resented many of the changes I was insistent upon. In addition to practicing for games and pep rallies, they were given character building activities. Rules were strictly enforced, and getting to be a cheerleader became something one earned, not a beauty and popularity contest. Grades and citizenship became as important as skills. Less focus was put on stage performance and more on all-around character and academic acumen. I wanted cheerleaders to be exemplary because, with their short skirts dotting the campus, they were so visible. I insisted that they be dressed alike, down to stud earrings only and ribbons only if all wore them. I wanted them to be thought of as a squad for boosting school spirit, not just pretty girls who stunned the crowd by jumping high, tumbling down the field, and climbing in dangerous stunts. I worked hard at eliminating the drama so often present among high school girls, and I encouraged them to love and respect one another on a daily basis. And oh yes, there was no more getting out of class to serve as escorts, guides, etc.

Interestingly enough, what I got were highly competent leaders of school spirit who were good students in class but also beautiful and skilled cheerleaders. Over a period of eight years, I had award winning cheerleaders who were also, for the most part, excellent role models for the whole school population. I took them to NCA cheerleading camps at Stephen F. Austin, Tarleton State, TCU, or SMU every summer where they earned top awards for spirit as well as skill. Many were selected as All-American cheerleaders, and many went on after graduation to work at NCA summer camps or to become Dallas Cowboy or college cheerleaders.

Even though our district discouraged participating at the state level, one year we competed and ranked high.

This was a great experience for me. Some of my memories include being given a bright blue wig to wear to pep rallies and being asked to present my then varsity squad on local television. I still play the tape the district made for me on occasion because it reminds me of so many good times. Most of my girls remember that I was quite a taskmaster when it came to practicing for camp as well as games. They say that my most remembered words are "Just one more time," which they all knew really meant "We will repeat it as many times as it takes to get it perfect."

I worked hard to make them a respected group of girls, and I believe I succeeded. I only gave up sponsorship when I was given honors and gifted and talented English classes that were more demanding of my time. I established some wonderful relationships with these girls, however, and even though this was in the early 1980's, I hear from many of them to this day.

The Birth of Senior Mentorship

After teaching the Gifted and Talented Language Arts program for several years, I realized that many of my students were having trouble deciding what path to follow post high school. Parents of my past students often called me, complaining when their children were switching majors, trying to find their right "fits." Many who were gifted in English were also gifted in their other core subjects. Not only were they gifted academically; many were gifted in the fine arts. A large percentage could have experienced successful careers in many areas, and they went off to college thinking, "What on Earth do I want to do?" Some were yielding to parental pressure because of no specific choices of their own.

Other problems I observed that seniors were having involved getting all their college application essays done, getting scholarship applications filled out, and just selecting the right colleges to attend.

About this time, I was involved in a course through

Texas A&M at Commerce that called for me to do an independent study. I chose to design a class for gifted and talented seniors that would solve some of these problems. Elaine Griffin, the then-English Coordinator for the school district, helped me with the curriculum and requirements that would allow students to get honors credit for the class. Once the plan was finalized, Elaine submitted it to the State Education Board, and it was approved.

This project is probably one of the achievements of which I am most proud of accomplishing. Students spent the first semester choosing schools to apply to, writing application essays, applying for scholarships, and taking career-matching tests. I brought in experts in all the fields the students had expressed an interest in so that they could listen to facts and ask questions they had concerning those fields. They then compiled a list of only those careers that they might be interested in pursuing.

By the end of the first semester, they narrowed the field of interest to one, and a person in that profession was chosen to serve as a mentor. A plan was then drawn up for getting the student exposed to everything possible concerning that profession. A total of eighty hours had to be spent under the tutelage of that mentor, but students were allowed to take time from class to fulfill this requirement. Each student kept a notebook, took notes, and kept up with activities during the first 12–15 weeks of that semester. At the end, a program was presented by the students that showed an audience of parents, friends, and community members exactly what had been accomplished by the mentorship experience. The student and mentor had planned this presentation together, but the actual presentation was by the student alone.

Interestingly enough, while I taught this class, almost as many students eliminated a possible career path due to their mentorship experience as it helped them to decide on one. Micah Pardun focused on dentistry, one of his interests, but his mentorship experience, while interesting and enjoyable, proved to him that law should be his focus. Chris Herrington's focus on Environmental Science helped him to decide on this for his major, and for several summers, because his mentor was so impressed with him, he returned to work at the City of Garland, where his mentor was employed. Not only did the mentorship class help him decide his future; it helped him pay for it. Either way, the objective was for students to have a firm decision made prior to entering college in order to save the time and money (not to mention the stress on both them and their parents) incurred by switching majors. I loved teaching this class, and at one time I even had two classes, one at the beginning of the day and one last period. Before I left North Mesquite, someone else had taken over teaching the class, and it is still being taught there today. When Horn finally got seniors, we also began a mentorship class. I'm not sure which high schools are now offering it, but all have expressed a desire to have it as a course offering. Several years ago, the course description changed; it is now available to honors students as well as gifted and talented students, but it still is an all-year course for which participants get honors credit.

SETTING THE STANDARD

Every time I composed a test, I took it before my students did. This allowed me to check for errors, and more important, it allowed me to check for validity. Almost always, I had to change some of the wording so that my instructions could be better understood.

The same was true for most of my creative project assignments. Although I never put together a trip scrapbook or a humanities notebook, I now wish I had forced myself to do that, too. However, I did do most of the writing that I assigned. When I assigned the writing of a poem, I wrote my own, usually at the same time they were writing theirs. I wrote my own essays; I wrote my own short stories. I always felt that modeling allowed me to understand better the process of teaching others the "how to" of writing.

During the course of a school year, I began requiring students to write letters to the editors of local newspapers. Many of my students published theirs in *The Dallas Morning News* and our local *Mesquite News*. I tried to submit some of my own ever so often so that they could see that I, personally, valued the art of forming educated opinions and sharing those opinions with others.

Over the years I've written many things that weren't worth saving, but I did pen a couple of short stories that I wrote for my granddaughters, a few poems for local contests, a few essays, some of which were published, and several letters to the editor. The following are some of the ones that I cherish the most. You will notice that I didn't say anything about their value except in relationship to me. None of them are great, but I still enjoy reading them every once in awhile.

I always encouraged my students to continue creative writing as well as writing letters to the editor. There is something about getting your thoughts onto paper that can be healing as well as entertaining. I hope they always write.

The following pieces are samples of what I wrote when I assigned my students to write.

"Anywhere, Anytime"
(A short story written for my granddaughter, Maci Choate)

Thank goodness the bell was ringing. Maci had sat in her English class feeling sorry for herself long enough. It was just that she still did not have a "man" in her life, and in spite of her dad's, "Love will be as easy as falling off a log for such a pretty girl," no one had really interested her since her sophomore year. She and Matt had some really good times that year, that is until he decided Shelly was more his type. She didn't think too much about it last year, but this year, she knew she would need a date for all the end-of-the-year senior activities, so she had been looking around, to no avail, all year. Now she had already missed two parties, and she really wanted to go to the senior prom, her very last high school dance.

As Maci left the building, she immediately decided to take the longer way home through the park. She had seldom had the opportunity to indulge herself due to her busy schedule, but "Today," she thought, "I deserve a break." This whole year she had been assigned so much to do around the house, so many places to go, or so much homework to get started on that she had been forced to take the quick way home every day, denying herself the pleasure she always found in nature.

As she sauntered down the lane into the park, she realized just how much she enjoyed walking this particular trail. As a young child, she and her dad had often walked it. She remembered one particular time, in fact, the very last time she had walked it with him. It was right before she entered Midtown High School. Her dad had developed tears in his eyes as they looked at the high school where she would soon be going. "You're not my baby anymore, Maci. You are going off to high school way too soon for me." While she didn't understand his tears at that point, maybe she did now. After all, she was even getting a little sentimental herself about leaving high school and entering the university. She and her parents had already decided that she would live in the dorm and not at home, and it was going to happen in just a few short months. She also felt excited about her impending freedom, though, in spite of her nostalgia.

Seeing a blue jay in a tree ahead, she decided to stop and watch it. She had taken so little time to enjoy nature, and bird watching was her favorite. Luckily, she spotted a slanted tree trunk, worn smooth by others who had stopped to rest. A mother blue jay was feeding her young, and it was almost as if she knew that Maci was watching. Every movement she made was slow and deliberate. Maci smiled, feeling as if she truly was the targeted audience for Momma Bird.

Engrossed, she failed to hear the runner, dripping in sweat, approach. "Do you mind if I share your log for a minute?" he asked.

"Of course not," she replied, wondering who this good-looking stranger was and why she had never seen him before.

"I'm on the university cross-country team, and today I decided to take an additional loop around the park. I've never come this way before and had no idea it would be such a long run."

"Oh, that explains why I've never seen you before. Is this your first year at the university? "

"Yes, it is," he answered. "By the way, my name is Chad Knight."

"Hi. I'm Maci Choate. I seldom come this way myself," she added. "I'm usually in such a hurry to get home from school that I don't take the time to go through the park, but I really love the walk." She silently added, "And, boy, am I glad I did today!"

"I'm an outside person myself. In fact, I'm about to take a group of boy scouts to Camp Grady Spruce as soon as school is out. One of my buddies' dad is a Scout Master and asked some of us to go as counselors. I'm looking forward to returning because I use to go every June when I was a scout."

"You're kidding. I went there in December for a Leadership Retreat. I'll bet you stayed in the part to the right as you enter, though. We stayed on the other side. I remember that they told us that scouts used the other side of the camp."

"If you went in December, then you didn't get to swim in the lake, did you? Possum Kingdom is the most beautiful lake for swimming that I have ever seen. You have got to go some time during the summer."

"Sounds like a winner," she smiled. It was nice having something in common with such a hunk. She felt even more convinced as they uncovered coincidence after coincidence concerning their interests, certain people they both knew, and surprisingly, some of their shared beliefs. Felt convinced? More like connected. They had even been at the same movie theater the weekend before; however, she had sat on the right side of the theater with her friends; he had been on the left. She felt a tinge of jealousy as he failed to reveal with whom he had seen the movie.

"Well, Mom is going to start worrying if I don't head home," she said as she reluctantly started to rise. Feeling a little light-headed, she began to fall backwards over the log. As he grabbed for her, she came up and into his arms for the best hug she had every experienced. "Um," she thought. "Dad knew what he was talking about. Love really is as easy as falling off a log."

"My Best Friend, Fate"
(A short story written for my granddaughter, Tori Anna Choate)

"What a dilemma," moaned Tori. "How am I ever going to decide on my date for the dance. Why, oh why, did they make it a Sadie Hawkins dance? I don't even know how to begin. I guess I could ask Matt. I really owe him an invitation since he took me to the football banquet in September. But Matt and I are just friends, and I think I want this to be more than just a 'friends night out' occasion."

"Maybe this is the time to get with Chad. Oops, that's probably out." She remembered that her mother had said just last week that no daughter of hers would be going with "college boys" while in high school, and Chad was a freshman in college. She would have to do some major convincing to get this to happen. "I don't know if I'm up to it," she thought.

"Tim would be a great date, but he is so shy. He would probably be too embarrassed to do any of the talking, and I could be stuck with coming up with things to say all night long. I don't think I have the stamina for this kind of date, yet he really is cute."

"Gary would be ideal, but I heard Jill plans on asking him. Maybe I should check with her because Gary really is a lot of fun to be around. Or maybe I should just ask him first. After all, 'All is fair in love and war.' Or so they say."

"Cole has been talking to me a lot in biology lately, and he's cute, too. I don't know anyone who has gone out with him, but it might be fun to go out with someone whom no one knows anything about. It would be a risk, though, 'cause he could be stuck on himself, or a real weirdo, or just plain boring, and I want so badly to have a really good time. This will be the last high school dance I ever attend, so I want it to be a night I'll remember forever."

After all this deliberating, Tori realized even more that she had a dilemma on her hands. How would she ever be able to decide, and time was quickly running out.

"Tori," called her mother. "There's a young man at the door for you."

Chills immediately ran down her spine. "Oh, my gosh! Fate has come to my rescue," she sputtered. "A bird in hand is worth five in the bush," she added. Then she descended the stairs to discover just who her date for the prom would be.

"Human Nature to a Fault"
(A personal response written during the inquiry into whether or not Supreme Court Justice Thomas should be approved to serve on the highest court of the nation)

It seems that lately I have seen some men
Who think that they can say just what they please,
No matter that they might offend someone.
Perhaps they can. A judge was just believed
Without a doubt. Do you suppose it's true
That human nature tends to brand all girls
As tempting Eves behind the sins of man?
Oh, please, dear God, create this world again
And blame the fall of woman on some man!

(Sonnets are hard to write, but with my help, students were able to see that they are a very specialized form of poetry. Those who got into them and understood how they are formed, had a ball. So did I. On the next page is another one I wrote. Writing these at the beginning of the school year threw the freshmen for a loop, but some caught on quickly and had as much fun as the rest of us.)

"The Irony of Summer"

I know that summer's nice when one is tired
And bored of homework, tests, and all school things.
You students think that when that last bell rings,
All pain and boredom surely will expire.

You say you want to lounge beside the pool
And go to shows and Starbuck's to chill out.
You are so ready for a break, you shout
Out loud and clear: "Goodbye to days of school!"

But so ironic is what happens next:
A month goes by and then you miss the place
Where all your friends meet daily and can talk.

The lessons for G/T are not complex,
And when you study hard, tests you do ace.
Perhaps school's not so bad as was first thought!

Remember When

Tire swings in big trees
And a barrel for rolling,
A jar of fireflies,
No one had a care.
Jacks and jump ropes,
Flashlights for patrolling,
Where are the toys
That used to be there?

Big spoons and tin pots,
So great for drumming.
Lids for cymbals,
A gourd to shake.
A comb and some paper,
Then add on-key humming.
Such simple items
A great band did make.

Mud pies in jar lids
With chinaberry filling,
Corncob dollies
With flowing silk hair,
Tree branch Y sling shots,
Fat flies for the killing,
Gone are the toys
That we used to share.

What is the reason?
We call it progressing.
Is cost so important
And cheap, so passe'?
Today's toys don't hold up,
Of this there's no guessing,
Yet yesterday's toys
We've taken away.

February 1999

March 15, 2001

Dear Editor:

When I tell people I am a high school teacher, the usual response is something like "How on earth do you handle today's degenerate teenagers?" While the behavior and tastes and values of teenagers have changed, so have the behavior, tastes, and values of our whole society. What hasn't changed is that teenagers still respect those who respect them, and adults still respect those who respect them.

I have great students who consistently respect me. These students are from every learning level—regular, honors, and gifted—and every socio-economic level. They are from single-parent homes as well as families with both parents. Most of these students listen to loud music and watch all kinds of television. Yet, these students consistently respect me, and I believe it is because I respect them.

Perhaps adults should recognize that once a child reaches high school, he should be looked at as just another adult, a young one but nevertheless an adult, a person with differing values and preferences, maybe, but nevertheless, an adult—an adult who also deserves to be respected.

Sincerely,
Linda Muhl

August 3, 1998
Dallas Child
Attention: Mailbox
4125 Keller Springs Rd.
Suite 146
Dallas, TX 75244

Re: "All Gambling Is Wrong" (August)

I find it difficult to believe that someone would consider a Christian radio station's pitch of "the seventh caller with the right answer gets the prize," gambling; however, Ms. Kelley obviously sees it not only as gambling but as "sin." Personally, I find it difficult to consider any situation where there is no loser as gambling. When I buy a ticket for a cake raffle fund-raiser to help sponsor children slated for a curriculum enhancing trip to New York, I feel that I am a winner even if I take no cake home. What is "sin" to Ms. Kelley may be charity in the minds of many of us.

In is definitely the reference to "sin" in this letter that really bothers me. To infer that "good luck" is evil (due to its connection to the word "Lucifer") seems a little absurd. I do, however, admire Ms. Kelley's standing up for what she believes. To say that gambling is wrong and then support the purchase of lottery tickets or seek entertainment at horse races is certainly exercising a double standard. Perhaps this is the most important part of the issue. What do we as parents want to teach our children about it? We (and other influential adults) must be aware that our actions speak louder than words. We should make sure our own values are firmly established concerning this controversial issue so that we can not only take a staunch position but model that belief for the young people we influence.

Sincerely,
Linda Muhl

August 13, 2001

Mesquite Bureau
Mesquite Morning News Section
The Dallas Morning News
18601 LBJ Frwy., Suite 240
Mesquite, TX 75150

Dear Editor:

As both a parent and a public school teacher, I am aware of how important parents are in the process of educating students. I am very thankful for all parents who realize this importance and send us young people who know how to behave and who want to learn.

When children are taught at home to value education and to have compassion and respect for others, teachers have more time to devote to the employment of effective teaching strategies rather than spending their time disciplining unruly students who have no desire to learn nor allow others to learn. I am fortunate that most of my students have parents who balance their parenting with both love and structure.

Unfortunately, this is not always the case. Way too many parents empower their children to the extent that their children are then able to "over-power" them. What is needed is more parents who are willing to give their children choices but who will also allow them to be accountable for their wrong decisions. This calls for "tough love," something many parents lack the courage to practice. Yet, the human tendency is to have NO preference for doing what is right when there is no significant, immediate consequence for making wrong decisions. Can we afford to continue to take this chance with our young people?

There is no limit to what students can learn when both parents and teacher fulfill their responsibilities for educating children. Parents must send us children who value education and who respect themselves and others. Teachers must educate themselves optimally in their subject matter and utilize effective strategies for teaching what students need to know in order to live happy and productive lives. It is a partnership we must constantly be mindful of and strive for if we love our children.

Sincerely,
Linda Muhl

August 4, 2007

Mesquite Star News
Mesquite, TX 75149

A submission for Viewpoints:

Calling All Adults. . .

Today's society is extremely lacking in the morals department. What has happened to honesty and integrity? In addition to reading about and hearing stories of the so-called criminal element committing rape, murder, theft, and abuse, it is not uncommon to hear that some of the high-profile people whom teenagers admire are less than admirable. The mentality seems to be "what I am doing is not wrong unless I get caught." Athletes who take steroids seem to think they are above the law. Even people in high places of our government seem to have the same attitude. What can we expect from our young people when we have sport figures, entertainers, businessmen, educators, political leaders, and even Presidents who mislead this country with a lack of truth and honor? Even some religious leaders appear to be less than "on the up- and-up" when they build multi-million dollar personal homes with public donations contributed for the Lord's work.

As a teacher, I hear stories of parents who call in and lie about absences in order to cover for their children who just don't want to come to school. Teachers and administrators are seeing less support and more confrontation from parents whose children misbehave during school hours. It is obvious that many parents are not "training" their children "in the way they should go" because there is rampant cheating on homework and tests, and students appear to have less and less control over their emotions, causing more confrontations and fights that disrupt education on a regular basis. At my school, as well as others in the district, the administrators have had to apply strong measures to insure that our campuses are safe, something we didn't have to worry about until the last few years.

Perhaps if our most visible public figures would exemplify character, and parents would be steadfast in their resolve to set good examples for their children, teenagers would not feel so justified in ignoring honesty and integrity when it comes to their own behavior. The educators I know and work with feel a strong sense of responsibility to be good role models for young people, but we cannot do it alone. We need help. This is not a request; it is a plea.

Sincerely,
Linda Muhl

This is the last poem I wrote for all my students, past and current.

ALWAYS AND EVER

How hard it is to say good-bye;
It's never an easy task.
Yet time has come
To say these words,
And this is all I ask. . .

Remember what I've told you:
"Get on that train-take flight!
Don't let one opportunity
Slip by you in the night."

If something is worth doing,
It's certainly worth doing well;
Presentation is the name of the game,
For words alone won't "sell."

Be kind to all those whom you meet,
For no one has the right
To hurt or maim another
By lacking keen insight.

Don't let your human failings
Damage your integrity.
Stand up and take your medicine
With all humility.

It's not like I've said these one time;
I've said them o'er and again.
I hope you'll always hear my voice
And then remember when. . .
I was your teacher for a year and more,
And I cared and wanted for you
A broad-based knowledge of many things
And a frame of reference, too.
I hope you remember to keep in touch
Through college and marriage—whatever.
For I'll always care and wonder about you;
I'll be your teacher forever.

Mrs. Muhl

VI

RETIREMENT

CELEBRATIONS LEADING TO MY RETIREMENT

I can't even begin to describe the days before my retirement. I am still amazed at what my students (current and former), their parents, my co-workers, my family, and my friends did to honor me as I retired from public school teaching. My eyes fill with tears every time I think of the many activities that took place those last few weeks.

The staff at my "home-away-from-home," John Horn High School, showed their love, respect, and appreciation to me with a reception held in the library. Thoughts from many with whom I had worked were displayed on a television monitor by the librarians, Karen Allen and Phyllis Grady. On the table were excellent punch and a great carrot cake baked by my co-worker, Brenda Gragg, not to mention my favorite flowers. Speakers Dr. Linda Henrie and former-student-then-fellow-teacher, Patrick Haney, made me cry with their memories and praise of my service. Gifts from individuals and an amazing group gift kept me shopping for months past the day, and I received many touching cards that are still valued beyond words. I was so overwhelmed that I might have forgotten some details, but I do know and remember how much I appreciated all the kind words and deeds connected with this reception.

My English department friends did something so special and meaningful to me. They each created an original page for a scrapbook that they presented to me. They also hand-wrote messages to me on quilt squares that were then pieced together to form a throw for my home. I still show it to everyone and read the messages on a regular basis. I had the best possible teachers in my department, and they continued to make my life easier and more pleasant all the time I served as the department head.

My close friends, Cathy and Andrew Bauer, made this time even more special by hosting a back-yard cookout in my honor. I loved visiting with this close-knit group, most of whom were chaperones for at least one of my student trips to New York City, Washington D.C., or Disney World. Again, words cannot express how I feel about this great group of friends' response to my retirement.

The huge retirement party that was arranged by parents of my students (both current and former) was the biggest shock of all. They brought my family members in early for a complete Italian meal prior to the celebration. They planned a program in the auditorium that was amazing. They arranged a reception afterward that left me speechless. And they gave me gifts that were just unbelievable. Among the gifts I received that night were gift cards, personal items, books, a Dell laptop computer (red so that I would not forget Horn), and a trip for two to England, Scotland, and Ireland. The amazing program featured students I had not seen in a while as well as current students. The talent displayed that night was exemplary. The speeches touched me deeply. The video surprised and delighted me. I just cannot say enough about this night. I truly felt like a queen (after all, I was wearing a tiara). But, it is the memories I will have for the rest of my life that were the greatest gift I received.

Presentation of Mrs. Linda Muhl and Mr. Drew Muhl
Escorted by Brian Rhodes
Presentation of Honors by Emily and Maggie Pieppenbrink

Welcome............................ Mark McSpadden
JHHS School Song............... Representatives of JHHS
NMHS School Song.............. Representatives of NMHS
Speaker .... Michelle Odemwingie
Song Performance.................. Matthew Montana
Speaker........................... Christian Rodriguez
Song Performance.................. Carlie Zimmerman
Speaker........................... Kim Beal
Song Performance.................. Nick, Rachel, and John Leos
Presentation of Scrapbooks........... Katie Wheeler and Helen Chatt
Song Performance.................. Justin Lott
Presentation of Warm Fuzzies...... Kylie Kovar and Lauren Vandiver
Song Performance.................. Choir Former Students
"I Will Remember You"
Speaker........................... Lauren Torenko Becker
Song Performance.................. Courtney Kilgore & Matthew Montana
Honors and Proclamation............ Helen Chatt and Lauren Gregory
Song Performance.................. Sarah Allen
Presentation of Gift................ Mackenzie Kilgore & Angela Kilgore
Speaker........................... Jeff Casper
Slide Show with Poetry Recitation.. Brian Hasley
Song Performance.................. All Current and Former Students
"Wind Beneath My Wings"

Response from Mrs. Muhl
Recessional of Mr. and Mrs. Muhl

Reception and Receiving Line in the JHHS Cafeteria

The Program

MY RETIREMENT SPEECH

I am so pleased to see that all of you students from North Mesquite have not forgotten me and that all of you Horn students are willing to listen to me one more time. Thank you all for coming.

What a tribute this has been! Never in all my life did I dream of what you, who organized this celebration, were doing at all those committee meetings. You have shocked, surprised, and greatly pleased me tonight. When asked what I wanted for this occasion, I merely said, "I want it to be a celebration, not a funeral," but I can truly say, if I died tonight, I would die happy.

What you see before you this evening—a seventy-year-old retiring teacher—is only what you have created: I am what I am because you, every person in this room tonight, has touched my life: my family, friends, parents, and students alike. I am but a reflection of your influence on me.

Twenty-nine years ago, I applied late and got hired

<u>one</u> day before school started. My assignment was to teach American and World History, my second teaching field, but that did not matter. I was ecstatic. I was realizing a dream—my dream of being a teacher.

Twenty-nine years later, I'm still a teacher. I think I will <u>still</u> be a teacher twenty-nine years from now. (Ha, ha)

Supreme and lasting joy—that is what teaching has given me and what I wish for each of you.

To my friends and family, thanks for supporting me in my pursuit and for loving me in spite of my sometimes "one-track mind." I have to tell you that although I can take no credit for it, I consider this part of my legacy: I am so proud of my family members who have chosen teaching as a profession: my son Kip, my daughter Sally, my daughter-in-law Linda, and my grandchildren Kristen, Daniel, Dustin, and Kris Ann. A special thank you goes to my role model as a teacher, my friend, my mentor, my sister, Nan, who without her strong influence and example as an excellent teacher herself, <u>I</u> might have achieved less. A special thank you goes to my husband. In spite of the fact that I could never convince him to grade a single paper, he has done everything else to make my teaching experience enjoyable. He has supplied every tool that the district did not furnish; he has sacrificed a lot of "we" time so that I could have all the "me" time needed to do the job my way; he has served as a sounding board for all my wild plans; he has accompanied me to school events; run errands for me (including bringing things to school that I have accidentally left at home); he has edited more than one of my handouts; and he has shared happy tears over the many wonderful and touching love notes and letters that I have received from you all throughout the years. I guarantee you that behind this teacher, there has been a good, no, a <u>very</u> good man. Thank you, Honey. And how can I not give a special thank you to my friends, my alter egos, my YoYo sisters, Lynne and Gay. Even my students know how important they have been to me as a teacher, accompanying us on every field trip and being the ones to go to when I'm not available. But their worth extends to my personal life, for they are also my soul mates.

To the parents of my students, current and former—let me praise you one more time. You have never interfered, never pressured, never criticized—just always supported everything I ever wanted for your children. You've willingly given your money, your time, your effort (you know, like at garage sales), your suggestions (and did I mention your money?) to support every opportunity I've dreamed up for your children. "Thank you" is not enough to give you in return, but please accept it along with my praise. You are the best!

To my students—former and current—I'm afraid I have no new advice. My messages to you have always been integrated into standard English curriculum. It is true that for every lesson on reading and writing, you've also gotten a heavy dose of life lessons. I'll bet that many of you can finish my sentences. In fact, let's just see:

So many opportunities will come only once in life, so make sure that you don't let life...

...pass you by like a train in the night.

There is something much more important than the grade on this test. Please, do not compromise...

...your integrity.

There is one thing you have to learn before you go to college if you want to be academically successful AND have fun, and that is to make sure that you first take...

...care of your business.

No matter how good your ideas are, no one will buy them if you don't...

...present them well.

Along the same lines concerning presentation, I have said one million times, no mixed...

...media.

Also, please do not use the wrong . . . and please do not use the wrong paper, which is...

...glue.

...construction paper.

Throughout my teaching ministry (that's what I call it), I have made decisions that due to some ironic coincidence, I

have taken it as God's approval of what I am doing.
I call this a...
...dove-on-my-shoulder experience.

Back to integrity: when I have told you that not only
is it important not to cheat off your neighbor, it is also
important that you cover up your answers in order to
protect his integrity. If you don't, I say that you are playing
the role of the . . . and who wants to play that role?
...devil.

Concerning outline, paper, and bibliography format, I have
referred you to an exemplary one that I furnished.
At NMHS, it was "just look at Jessica's";
at Horn, it is "just look at..."
...Julia's.

Once a Muhlet, ...
...always a Muhlet.

I will always be your...
...teacher.

So much for life lessons.

Now, my students (former and current), if I have also:

—endowed you with greater ease for reading

challenging books,

—given you a love and appreciation for the fine arts,

—shown you how to write an effective paper,

—convinced you of the importance of making allusions,

—taught you the importance of camaraderie,

—convinced each of you of your own value and uniqueness,

—and pointed you on the path to serene and lasting joy,

then I will consider my job done, for these were my major objectives.

I can then say goodbye to you tonight as the teacher in front of the classroom, but let me tell you this: I will always be looking over your shoulder, and you will always be in my heart.

There is a legend that a small boy once walked up to Michelangelo and asked him why he was chiseling away at a chunk of marble. His reply was, "I am merely letting the angel inside go free." That is what I have tried to do for all of you, my students: chisel away until your spirit is free. I hope I have succeeded.

VII

POST RETIREMENT

SINCE THEN

I have to tell you a little about our trip, first. When we got to the lake country of England, we realized that we needed a car to see the beautiful countryside. As soon as this was determined, like magic, an English couple, Brenda and Alan Wilbraham, who were there for a holiday asked if we would like to accompany them for a day of sightseeing. This was a wonderful and unexpected extra that we had not planned for, and their kind hospitality made that part of our trip special.

A prior student of mine from North Mesquite, Allison Schmitz, once told me that her mother, Mary, was from Ireland. I called Mary, a nurse at Vanston Middle School, to ask her about sites we should see when in her home country, but because she had been removed from there so long ago, she immediately referred me to her brother and sister-in-law, Seamus and Mary Enright, who insisted that we stay with them while in Ireland. They were on holiday from their jobs, so they took us all over the island and gave us a tour that most people would not get. We got to visit County Mayo, from where my husband's grandmother came to America. We saw so many places that we had heard about, and we truly fell in love with the beautiful countryside. They made our trip even more special.

In addition to using the tickets, reservations, and the spending money given to me at my retirement party for our fabulous trip to the British Isles, I have been busy doing so many things that I never had time to do before. I have spent much more time with my sisters and my husband. I have finished hooking a rug that I started about 35 years ago. I have started tons more creative projects, too numerous to even list. And I have entertained about once a month for the last year.

I guess staying busy has been good for me; however, sometimes I think I must slow down and enjoy life more. Not only have I never gotten my fill of teaching; I still love to learn. I have tried ceramics painting for the first time, and although the box has not been opened, I just bought a sewing machine, my first ever. I have great plans for using that machine, but I just have not gotten around to making those plans happen. I really want to take some art lessons, but maybe that will have to wait until I can finish some of the things I have already started.

In spite of all this "busyness," I still miss my spot in front of the classroom.

Notes on Being Retired

I never wanted to be an ex-anything. As an ex-wife (after being married for thirteen years), I felt lonely and defeated. The few years I was an ex-Baptist (Drew and I attended the Presbyterian church for several years when we first married), I felt misplaced and disoriented . As an ex-employee (I quit my job to take care of four children when Drew and I married), I often felt disorganized, empty, and lacking routine.

But these feelings—lonely and defeated, misplaced and disoriented, disorganized, empty and lacking routine— were nothing like what I felt when I retired from teaching and to some degree, still feel. . .in spite of the fact that I've read numerous books, discussed books, shared books, and even serve as a sponsor for a reading club at my sister's senior living apartment complex, . . . in spite of having ten parties and planning two more, . . . in spite of organizing and participating in several community service projects, . . .in spite of planning and organizing two trips (one to New

York and one to Granbury), . . . in spite of hemming many napkins and making many fleece blankets, . . .in spite of going to four markets having eleven jewelry shows, . . .in spite of planning and organizing a family reunion, . . .in spite of going to England, Scotland, and Ireland, . . .in spite of joining and becoming more involved in church, . . .in spite of having two garage sales, . . .in spite of getting our personal affairs in order, . . .and in spite of writing this book.

Retiring was definitely the biggest adjustment I have ever made. Even when my mother died, she had been sick long enough to give me sufficient time to get ready for her death. It still hurt, but I realized that her death was really a blessing because she was no longer in pain. When my sister, Nan, left Dallas to live in Tennessee and then Mississippi, I felt like part of my heart left town, but seeing her happy in her new life helped ease the loss I felt. In fact, accepting every change that has occurred in my life has been hard, but nothing like adjusting to no longer being able to stand before a class and teach. I was in my element. I was doing what I was supposed to do. I was fulfilling my job on Earth. Staying busy has helped, but I don't think I will ever stop yearning for a student audience.

People ask me why I don't substitute. Substituting is nothing like teaching. Doing that job would just make me miss teaching even more. People have suggested that I teach other groups, so I am considering teaching a group of adults at church. I enjoy making presentations, such as the short lesson in art appreciation that I presented to the Mesquite

Symphony Debutantes, and I will continue to do those kinds of presentations when I am asked. Serving on the Mesquite Education Foundation Board and the Community Education Advisory Council are two new responsibilities that I have taken on, and I enjoy having this on-going connection to education. However, even though all of this involvement has helped, the ache is still there. I think it will be there until I die.

Once a teacher, always a teacher! I just can't get it out of my mind. . .or my heart.

Fifty Things I Miss About Teaching
(And There Are More)

1. Being in front of a classroom full of students awaiting my message of the day
2. Taking them on local field trips, like the Arboretum
3. Taking them to Disney World, Washington, D.C., and New York City
4. Taking them to plays, operas, ballet performances
5. Having pens that matched my outfits
6. Planning symposiums, like those on art appreciation or leadership
7. Taking them on a Leadership weekend and providing other leadership training
8. Giving the "integrity" speech
9. Exchanging warm fuzzies
10. Interacting with given students by playing "the devil's advocate"
11. Sharing my own life experiences with my students
12. Helping individual students through personal crises
13. Getting to meet parents of incoming freshmen each spring

14. Showing off my students' trips and humanities appreciation scrapbooks
15. Displaying their letters to the editor in colorful display
16. Modeling the writing of poetry
17. Teaching poetry scansion
18. Teaching grammar
19. Discussing classics
20. Hearing deep and insightful statements on difficult texts from individual students
21. Observing "ah ha" moments when students finally understood difficult concepts
22. Hearing and watching my students skilled in the performing arts perform on stage
23. Watching my student athletes perform, reading about them in the newspaper
24. Guiding my students when they had difficult decisions to make
25. Having my seniors stop by occasionally for a hug
26. Answering my door at home to students who had procrastinated
27. Hearing a shy student contribute willingly and confidently for the first time
28. Witnessing the love my students had for one another
29. Keeping parents informed via email and handouts
30. Sharing noteworthy magazine and newspaper articles with them
31. Laughing and crying, whatever the circumstance, with my students
32. Enjoying the camaraderie felt among teachers

33. Observing the camaraderie felt among gifted students
34. Helping students understand their parents
35. Getting students to see the other side (of problems with other teachers)
36. Grading tests (at least the first half) After that, it could get a little old
37. Seeing their creativity at work (colors, designs, themes, motifs)
38. Introducing brand new information
39. Seeing grade improvement
40. Attending award ceremonies
41. Sanitizing the table tops
42. Putting up the thematic bulletin board at the beginning of the year
43. Seeing students laugh at their own mistakes instead of being embarrassed
44. Hearing students realize how much they have learned over the course of their three years
45. Seeing students express compassion for others by participating in benevolent activities
46. Seeing a vertical team truly work well together
47. Seeing students volunteer to fill out absentee forms without my asking
48. Implementing the pass-out process without calling out names and seeing it work like clock-work
49. Having a student make 100 on "tub corrections"
50. Getting a thank you from a student who had me write a letter of recommendation

What I Couldn't Say in the Classroom Then But Now Can

I will be the first to say that a teacher's job is to educate his/her students, which involves sharing everything known about a given subject, in a way that it can be understood and remembered for application. Values about living life should be the main responsibility of parents and religious leaders.

With that said, I never figured out how to hide my own values, and I believe that by my modeling certain values, they often "slid onto" my students. I admitted my own Christianity the only safe way I knew how: by beginning some sentences with, "I can only speak from a Christian standpoint, . . ." or "Now Christians would say. . ." and other such phrases. But I never tried to overstep the boundaries imposed on me. I never witnessed for Christ, even though I sometimes thought that He is exactly what a student needed. I truly believed that the "supreme and lasting joy" that I wanted for all my students had to include Christ. I did try to live an exemplary life. I was very conscious of ever being an example for my students.

Ethics was a large part of my curriculum: no cheating, no hurting anyone's feelings, being responsible, apologizing—all these were stressed almost daily in the front of every classroom I ever stood before. My students knew that I believed that they should always respect their parents. I will never forget being in a conversation with a student and her mother when all of a sudden, the student began berating her mother. I grabbed her arm and told her, "You WILL NOT talk to your mother this way in my presence." She quickly apologized, and we later had several conversations about how she could disagree with her mother without being disrespectful.

This example brings me to another subject. Gifted students often have their own ideas about how things should be and don't mind telling others. Sometimes this appears disrespectful, even if it is not intended to be. I always tried to get across that there is a method to making this happen that sometimes even involves convincing others that it is their idea. One should never force his ideas on others; he should take his time to build his case and then approach the subject in a positive, respectful manner. If students would exercise this technique, one of "I need your help" rather than "You are wrong," there would be very few teacher-student problems. If a student disagrees with a teacher, he should approach with an attitude of "I need your help because I don't understand something you said. Could you please explain it?" Then he will get the help he needs and wants. If he approaches the teacher with "You graded my paper wrong," he is going to see a very defensive attitude, and he will, more often than not, fail to succeed at getting the correction or information that he wants from that teacher.

I also told my students that this tactic works with parents, too: "If you plot your course well and enter the conversation with a positive attitude, you can have more control over parental response. If you demand that your parents do something, they will immediately balk, but if you convince them of the merits of such action, they will love to comply to your wishes." Parents basically are very pro-child. We love to do things our children want us to do. If it is in our power, we will do whatever it takes, within the realm of good parenting, to maintain a good relationship with our children.

So, now I can say what I could never say in the classroom. My style of teaching, my way of mentoring, my way of relating, my way of living and sharing my life with others is my testimony. It is my evangelistic contribution to living a Christian life. Regardless of their religious affiliation, I can only hope that all my students find the "serene and lasting joy" that comes with living in sync with God.

THE "WHO"

The "Who" didn't start out as the "Who." It started out as a group of friends who got together every month or so for a social outing. At first, we met for a Christmas party, and because it was Christmas, we decided to bring decorated shoe boxes filled with gifts for needy teenagers who just might not have a very merry Christmas. I learned about this need from my friend who was once associated with Mesquite Social Services, Jana Kovar. While I was still teaching at Horn, she told me that many people donated household items for adults and an assortment of gifts for children at Christmastime but that rarely did they receive anything appropriate to give teenagers. My students did these teenage gift boxes one Christmas, and because it was so appreciated, I asked my friends if this appealed to their giving spirit. Of course, they said it did, so this became our first community service project.

Another time that we met, we provided gifts for newborns and their mothers who are served through a "safe house" that I found out about from the director of Mesquite Social Services. At that meeting, we even completed previously cut-out fleece baby blankets, which we took to this same organization. Another project was to bring as many coloring books and boxes of Crayolas as we could collect. As a result, over 250 of each were given to both Mesquite Social Services and Sharing Life for distribution at their discretion.

After we realized that we had become a service organization (as much as a social gathering), we decided that we needed a name. We were always being asked, "Now who is donating these items?" which was difficult to explain. Someone came up with the name, the "Who," which stands for "Women Helping Others." We all liked it, so that is what we are now called.

A conversation that I had with the principal of Gray Elementary School, Karen Lloyd, who just happens to be the mother of one of my former students from North Mesquite, Chelsea Pearce, inspired our last project. When I asked her how she was adjusting to a move from Beasley Elementary to Gray, she told me that it had been a great year. She went on to tell me that there was one thing that really bothered her about the children at Gray: that there were so many first graders who had no book at home to read and call their own. This gave me the idea, and the group was very receptive to meeting this need. We got a reading list for first graders from the Gray librarian, and followed up by asking others to help us. All together, we collected almost two hundred new books to be used as gifts for these young students. Then, with the help of some more individuals and student groups at Horn, we were able to do the same for Floyd Elementary, whose principal, Kim Broadway, also happens to be the mother of one of my former students, Leland Sawyer.

Who knows what the "Who" will do next? We will continue to help both needy groups and individuals that we hear need our help. We've gotten to the point that our service projects give us just as much pleasure as the food and fellowship we share each time we meet. For this reason, we will continue to help both groups and individuals in our area who need our help.

This reminds me of something that once bothered me. When I realized how good it made me feel to give and to do for others, I gave and did even more. Then I felt guilty. I thought that if I was benefitting more than the receiver, that was pretty selfish motivation on my part. Eventually I realized that this was not the case. God said that when we do for others, we also do for Him. It is because of this that He blesses both givers and receivers equally.

In Closing

I have so many people to thank for helping me get my thoughts down on paper. Certainly everyone who has ever touched my life is a part of who I am, so every association has created the experiences I have shared on these pages.

More specifically, I owe my sister Nan a big thank you for editing every chapter so willingly. I really appreciate those who wrote such nice things about me and this book in the Forward: my good friend and co-worker for years, Gay Bennett; a former student, Emily Southerland; and a parent of two former students, Doug Hall. A special thanks also goes to Cathy Hall, the illustrator for the cover. And because all of my students over the years are the major inspiration for my writing the book, I would like to say thank you to each of you personally. I wish I could have named each one, but that was an impossibility. I mentioned a few to get my points across, not because they were my "favorites." Those who know me well know that I always have loved all my students the same.

I could never thank my husband, Drew, enough. In addition to seeing that we have had a wonderful personal life together and security for the future, he definitely made me a better teacher during those twenty-eight years I taught. Not only did he pay for my college education; he paid for every extra "gizmo" that I felt like I needed in my classroom. I am probably the only teacher in the world who has gotten birthday gifts of an electric hole punch, a lectern, and filing tubs, but because I wanted these things, Drew got them for me. I cannot tell you how many gift certificates he has given me to Office Max, Book Stop, and the teacher's store that is now out of business. He bragged to everyone about my accomplishments, clipped out every mention of my name in the newspaper, sent copies to all of our out-of-town relatives, and he always thought and told others that I was the best teacher in the world. This is the ultimate gift any husband can bestow on his wife. Oh, how I love my soul mate.

This is it. I have taxed my brain enough for one year. If you who undertake the reading of this book enjoy it even half as much as I have enjoyed writing it, then it is worth all the effort.